Published since 1897 MAGAZINE

RAILWAY ANNUAL 96

WORLD TRAINS AND WHERE TO SEE THEM

APL

ACKNOWLEDGEMENTS

This book was created for APL by Dave Roberts and David Jefferis, who wish to thank all who have provided assistance, including:

Bill Alborough, TEFS Ltd
Philip Atkins, National Railway Museum Library
Hugh Ballantyne
Simon Brown, Cityrail, Sydney
David Cox, TNT Harbourlink, Sydney
Stephen Drew, Senior Curator, California State Railroad Museum
Colin Garratt
GEC Alsthom/CAV SNCF/JJD
David Haydock
Gerard Isvi
Sue Jenkins
Oliver Lewy, Brush Traction
Llangollen Railway Society members
Caroline Mackaness, Museum of Sydney
Paul Quinn, Inchicore Depot, Iarnrod Eireann
David Rogers
Danny Sheehan, Australian Railway Historical Society
Shed staff at the Isle of Man Steam Railway
SNCB Belgian Railways
Swedish Railways
Ron White

Photographs supplied by:
Hugh Ballantyne
Doug Birmingham
Shirley Burman
Dick Campbell
Bernard Collardey
Colour-Rail, Amersham
Mike Danneman
Eurotunnel
John Galton
Antony Guppy
GW Travel Ltd
David Haydock
David Jefferis
Central Railway of Japan
Fred Kerr
Milepost Library
Millbrook House Library
WL Moore
Malcolm Ranieri ARPS
Dave Roberts
David C Rogers
GEC Alsthom
Brian Robbins
James Robins
Quadrant Picture Library
WA Sharman
Spectrum Colour Library
Swedish Railways and Industrifotografen AB
TNT Harbourlink
RJS Wiseman

Hiawatha diagram by:
James Robins/Andromeda Oxford Ltd
Additional picture research:
Kay Rowley Associates

Dtp maps: Gavin Page
Colour repro: David Bruce Graphics, London
Printed by: New Interlitho Spa, Milan

Published by:
Annuals Publishing Ltd
One High Street
Princes Risborough
Bucks HP27 0AG
under licence from IPC Magazines Ltd

© IPC Magazines Limited 1995

ISBN 1-899107-05-3

Picture above: British 2-8-0T on freight charter near Quorn, Leicestershire.
Opposite: Spain's AVE high speed train.
Inside front cover picture: General-Electric Dash-9 No 612 leads a mixed freight descending through the Cajon Pass, California.
Title page: Le Shuttle loco in the Channel Tunnel.

CONTENTS

INTRODUCTION

Welcome to *Railway Magazine Annual 96*.
Here you will find a pot-pourri of locomotives large and small, collected from around the world. Thanks to the Channel Tunnel and the ever-expanding steam preservation movement, more and more people are becoming interested in railways. This annual is their ideal companion – not only is it an absorbing reference book for seasoned enthusiasts, but it also makes a good introduction for newcomers to the railway scene.
Within these full-colour pages you will find a cross-section of British and international locomotives old and new – from the *Rocket* of 1829 to the ultra high-speed types representing the cutting edge of today's technology.
But the book is not just for 'armchair enthusiasts'. For those of you who want to see the real thing, we have included details of where the locos and trains can be found – even those in remote corners of the world!
As well as the trains, we have included some enjoyable features – 'Great Rail Journeys' describes a trio of glorious runs, 'Models and Memorabilia' looks at the collectables scene, while 'Rail: The World Changer' looks at the past and the way railways developed. 'Into the Future' predicts what trains will be like in the 21st century, and finally 'Rail Records' and 'Technical Terms' round off the book with some useful (and fascinating!) facts.

All the best,

Nick Pigott
Editor, *Railway Magazine*

Flying Scotsman *at Llangollen, Wales.*

MAINLAND EUROPE

The continent of Europe has a variety of railway systems, nearly all state-owned. France and Germany were among the first to start building railways; Greece left it until early this century. Not only were several main gauges used, but a network of narrow-gauge lines, relatively uncommon in Britain, served even small villages in most countries. Those narrow-gauge lines that remain are mostly aimed at tourists; even so, in the Pyrenees and Alps there is engineering as spectacular as anything on a main line. Europe has rarely been free of war, but there has always been international running, and various EU countries are now benefiting from the rapid expansion of high-speed lines, including, via the Channel Tunnel, Britain. The eastern half of Europe is in a period of modernisation after decades of stagnation under communism, but the survival of large numbers of main line steam locos that were in service until recently has proved a great attraction for enthusiasts.

Picture above shows Sweden's successful X2000 tilting train.

CLASS 141R 'L'AMERICAINE' 2-8-2 – FRANCE

► *This superbly-restored loco belongs to the 'Association de la 141R 420' which operates various enthusiast tours from Clermont-Ferrand.*

TECHNICAL DETAILS

The 2-8-2 141R was built in North America in several factories, including those of Lima, Alco, Baldwin, the Montreal Locomotive Works and the Canadian Loco Works, Kingston, Ontario. The total weight varied from 187.5 tonnes to 188.25 tonnes, depending on the delivery batch. Overall length 24.13m (78ft 5in). Most were coal-fired, but a second batch of 640 were oil-burners.

French locomotives up to World War II were known for their very high efficiency, gained at the cost of complex compounding systems needing great skill to operate and maintain. To help re-establish itself after that war, SNCF had to buy a rugged, simple type from abroad, and it chose an American 2-8-2 design (in Continental notation, 1-4-1). By 1948 this one class, of which 1,323 were delivered (17 locos were lost in a shipwreck), was handling nearly half of France's rail traffic volume. Having only two cylinders and rudimentary wheel balancing, they were limited to 100 km/h (62 mph) to conserve the track. Even so, crews enthused about 'les Americaines' and their ease of maintenance more than made up for a hefty appetite for fuel, whether coal or oil. Several 141Rs are currently preserved in working order, as befits a classic type that was in service until the 1970s.

WHERE TO SEE IT The National Railway Museum at Mulhouse, Alsace, has at least two 141Rs which run excursions from time to time. For No 1126, based in Toulouse, telephone 0033 61 15 78 07. For information on No 420 at Clermont-Ferrand, write to BP 7, 63830 Durtol, France.

CLASS CC 7100 – FRANCE

► *CC7106 hauling a car train.*

TECHNICAL DETAILS

The first production batch of Class CC 7100 Co-Co electric locos was made in 1952 by Alsthom-Belfort and Fives-Lille. A total of six traction motors gave 3,492 kW (4,682 hp) with a 1.5 kV ac overhead supply. Of 60 locos made, including two prototypes built in 1950, 18 were still running in 1994. By Autumn 1995, CC 7107 had covered over 8.5 million km (5.3 million miles).

In the 1950s France's SNCF investigated the feasibility of running electric expresses at up to 200 km/h (125 mph). The fast electric 7100 class, first produced in 1952, was a candidate for speed trials. These culminated in two records that were far above regular speeds achieved at the time. On 28 March 1955, locomotive CC 7107 reached a record 326 km/h (202.6 mph) south of Bordeaux; the next day, BB-class loco No 9004 bettered this with 331 km/h (205.7 mph). The records being within five per cent of each other, both locos were credited with the higher speed. The locomotives, and the 100-tonne train they pulled, were extensively modified and streamlined for the trials. The 1,500 volt ac power supply was increased to 1,875 volts and power output of the locos was about 8,933 kW (12,000 hp), which is more than that of both the power cars of a present-day TGV. The 7100 class has another claim to fame – the oldest survivors are now 45 years old, and with reconditioning some may yet reach half a century of main line service.

WHERE TO SEE IT Several 7100s, including No 7107, are based at Avignon. They are being gradually withdrawn , but the class may just make it into the 21st century. Record-breaker BB 9004 is at the French National Rail Museum at Mulhouse.

EUROSTAR – FRANCE/BRITAIN

▲ *Eurostar near the French town of Belfort.*

To make best use of the Channel Tunnel link, a new generation of very fast passenger trains has been developed. Eurostar is based on the French TGV, but also operates on British third-rail 750 volt and Belgian 3000 volt dc. Eurostar's British-designed body and cab are new, and 18-coach formations require extra power bogies in the coaches next to the power cars. The initial fleet of 38 trains includes seven 14-car 'beyond-London' units, for journeys to Britain's regions. Scheduled time between London and Paris is presently about three hours, London to Brussels 15 minutes longer. New links on TGV/Eurostar routes should enable train journeys at 300 km/h (186 mph) between Europe's main cities by the year 2000.

WHERE TO SEE IT
Between London Waterloo, Paris Gare du Nord, and Brussels Midi. TGV Nord-Est line parallels the A1 motorway for some way, allowing rail and road speeds to be compared. In West London, trains are serviced at North Pole Depot, Old Oak Common (no public access). For bookings, ring local agents or Eurostar direct on 0345 300 003. For information only call 0891 515 477. Using these numbers, you can book rail travel to 5,000 European destinations.

TECHNICAL DETAILS
The first Eurostars were built in 1992-93 by GEC Alsthom. Each set has a power car and seven or nine coaches; two sets make up a train. Power supply 25 kV ac overhead, 3,000 volt dc overhead or 750 volt dc third rail. Power-car wheel arrangement Bo-Bo+Bo. Length overall for an 18-coach train is 393 m (1,289 ft). Maximum cruising speed 300 km/h (186 mph).

TGV – FRANCE

▶ *A 300 km/h (186 mph) TGV Reseau prepares to leave Gare du Nord, Paris. The TGV series has been extremely successful, not only in France, but in export markets too, with many orders from other countries.*

In 1981, SNCF opened its first new main line since 1928 (over half a century!), to carry passengers between Paris and Lyon at up to 270 km/h (168 mph). The TGV 'Train a Grande Vitesse' (high speed train) developed for this service was a lightweight rake of articulated coaches with a highly streamlined power car at either end. There was no provision for tilting on tight curves as the specially-made line was built with none. Success on this first route (competing air flights were severely hit) has enabled the TGV network to expand through the 1980s and 1990s to serve many cities, including Bordeaux, Berne, Geneva, Lille and Brussels, and to connect with the Channel Tunnel. Standard maximum speed on later lines is 300 km/h (186 mph), but earlier attempts with TGVs led to far higher speeds. On 18 May 1990, a modified TGV-A with four coaches achieved 513.3 km/h (320 mph), a speed likely to stay an all-time record for conventional rail traction.

WHERE TO SEE IT Original TGVs run between Paris and Lyon, and on to Geneva and Berne, among other places. TGV-A routes include Paris-Bordeaux and Rochelle; TGV-R runs between Paris-Lille and Brussels. SNCF train information is available in the UK on 0891 515 477.

TECHNICAL DETAILS

TGV-Reseau (Network) uses the same motors and bogies as Eurostar, but with only eight coaches and two Bo-Bo power cars per train. Power supply (France) 25 kV ac, (Belgium and Italy) 3 kV ac. The latest trains can also use the Dutch 1.5 kV system. TVM 430 cab-signalling equipment and auto train control are fitted, with functions monitored by computer. Drivers have radio contact with other trains and signal centres.

CLASS 12 4-4-2 — BELGIUM

◄ *Belgium's fine Class 12 at speed near Tilburg.*

TECHNICAL DETAILS

Class 12 4-4-2 Atlantic. Built in the 1930s by Cockerill, Seraing in Belgium. Inside cylinders were used to minimise oscillation. The driving wheels were 2.1 m (82.75 in) in diameter and steam pressure 18 kg/sq cm (256 psi). Eight tonnes of coal were carried, with a water load of 24,000 litres (5,280 galls). Length 21.19 m (69 ft 6.25 in).

The six Belgian National Railway Class 12 locomotives were both the last 4-4-2 Atlantics and the last inside-cylinder express engines ever built. Developed to haul trains the 121 km (71 miles) between Brussels and Ostend in exactly an hour, including a stop at Bruges, these stubby-looking streamliners were cleared to run at 140 km/h (87 mph), which they easily maintained with up to five coaches. One loco reached 165 km/h (102.5 mph) with this load, and from the spring of 1939 until war broke out in September, the Brussels-Ostend express was the world's fastest scheduled train at an average of 121 km/h (75 mph). The post-war electric trains which replaced them on the route were actually 11 minutes slower. One Class 12 loco, No 12.004, is preserved in working order by SNCB.

WHERE TO SEE IT The last survivor of the Class 12 streamliner type is shedded at Louvain (Leuven), east of Brussels.

REGIO RUNNER — HOLLAND

TECHNICAL DETAILS

French-built Regio Runner three or four-car units are fitted with electrical systems by Holec-Riddekerk, a Dutch firm. Bo-Bo power cars at either end develop 1,608 kW (2,090 hp) from overhead supply at 1,500 volts dc. Top speed is 160 km/h (100 mph) A three-car unit can carry 275 passengers, a four-car 372. Trains usually consist of more than one unit.

The Dutch rail system, under the Nederlandse Spoorwegen (NS) banner, was largely rebuilt after World War II to become one of the world's finest networks. All main lines are electrified, and it was decided at an early stage to make most passenger trains self-propelled, using locomotives mainly for freight. Double-deck trains proved so successful for commuter and inter-city traffic in the densely-populated Randstad area that a new fleet of double-deck electric multiple units, the Regio Runners, has been ordered. NS plans on doubling its passenger traffic by the year 2000, and the spacious Regio Runners, with their air-conditioning systems and mini-lifts for snacks trolleys, have great user appeal. Orders so far are for 34 three-car and 47 four-car units. They are built by the Talbot company in Aix-la-Chapelle, the second trailers for the four-car trains being supplied by de Dietrich of Niederbronn.

WHERE TO SEE IT Regio Runners operate an hourly service between Amsterdam and Vlissingen , via den Haag, Rotterdam and Roosendaal.

▲ *The stylish double-deck Regio Runners of Dutch Railways offer fast and frequent inter-city services.*

X2000 – SWEDEN

▲ *Coaches tilt on the X2000, but the power car (under the bridge's steel arch in this picture) stays upright on bends.*

One of Europe's newer high-speed trains, X2000 has done much to revive the flagging fortunes of Swedish Railways. The brief was tough – a train to operate on existing lines, many of them single-track, at up to 200 km/h (125 mph) in temperatures from -30°C to +30°C. Tilting was essential to allow curves to be taken comfortably at speed, and a further refinement was the 'soft' bogie, in which individual axles pivot to follow curves, reducing flange friction and oscillation. The first of 36 X2000s entered service in September 1990, reducing the 456 km (283 miles) Stockholm-Gothenburg run from over four hours to just three. Seating in the trains is standard at three-abreast and all are headphone-equipped; meals, newspapers, telephone and fax are all-inclusive in business class. Passenger numbers have risen sharply – over half Sweden's inter-city travellers now take the train. A second batch of 14 units for regional services, designated X2-2, have only four trailer cars.

WHERE TO SEE IT X2000s operate at present on the Stockholm-Gothenburg and Stockholm-Malmo routes. When upgrading and new lines are completed by the turn of the century, services will extend to Copenhagen in Denmark.

TECHNICAL DETAILS

X2000 is built by ABB's Swedish division. Trains have a power car and five coaches, the last being a driving trailer. Overhead 15 kV ac supply drives two traction motors in each bogie of the Bo-Bo power car. Motion sensors and a computer in the leading car tell coaches in sequence when and how much to tilt on their hydraulic jacks. Units can be coupled to make longer trains. Maximum test speed 276 km/h (171 km/h).

CLASS P36 4-8-4 – RUSSIA

▶ *A gleaming blue P36. This loco is maintained in working order, ready to haul rail tours through Russia.*

TECHNICAL DETAILS

The P36 has two cylinders, and driving wheels 1.85 m (72.8 in) in diameter. Weight of the coal-burner (there were oil-burners, too) is 264 tonnes. Russian track gauge is 1.52 m (60 in), and locos and stock on it can be up to 5.28 m (17 ft 4 in) high. A loco filling such a loading gauge could be too heavy for the track, so Soviet locos tend to be tall and slim, some with a casing for steam pipes and equipment atop the boiler.

Apart from a French prototype, Europe has produced only two classes of the 'ultimate' steam express layout, the 4-8-4 Northern type. Spain built just ten, but the former Soviet Union had the largest fleet of Northerns in the world, totalling at least 250. The first P36, resembling the 1930s JS-class but with an extra pair of rear carrying wheels (to reduce axle loading from 20 to 18 tonnes) was built at the Kolomna works near Moscow in 1953. Production began the next year, lasting until 1956. It was a mod-ern, well-equipped machine, with roller bearings throughout, mechanical stoking for the coal version, and a fully-enclosed cab with full-depth doors, essential for ultra-cold Russian winters. Painted green or light blue, P36s hauled prestige expresses, notably over non-electrified parts of the Trans-Siberian line.

WHERE TO SEE IT For tours hauled by P36s, including a Trans-Siberian special, contact GW Travel, 0161 928 9410. This company also organises rail tours in the Caucasus. Splendid stuff!

CLASS OL49 2-6-2 – POLAND

▶ Polish Ol49 No 27, photographed at Sierpe. Some of these mixed-traffic locos are still in service.

Poland is the last country in Europe to operate steam in regular main line service. Having, until recently at least, cheap labour and huge supplies of coal but little oil, Polish State Railways opted to keep steam for as long as it made economic sense. However, electrification is now widespread, and diesels have taken over branch line working. Steam is reduced to a few 'museum sheds', of which Wolsztyn is the foremost, maintaining an active steam fleet for branch line working in 1995. Freight traffic is seasonal, with Polish and ex-German 2-10-0s finding much work during the sugar-beet harvest. Wolsztyn (pronounced 'Volshtin') maintains Poland's last Prussian P8 and a magnificent Pt47 2-8-2 express passenger locomotive for enthusiast specials, but the mainstay of its fleet is the Ol49 mixed-traffic 2-6-2, which works some local passenger services.

WHERE TO SEE IT Wolsztyn is on the main north-south line from Szczecin to Wroclaw. It may not survive as a steam depot long after the 150th anniversary of Polish Railways in September 1995, so if you want to visit, go soon, before all the steam locos are retired or relocated!

CLASS P8 4-6-0 – GERMANY

◀ This German Federal Railways Class 38 No 382 was photographed at Horb am Neckar in 1972, while still in service.

By general reckoning the most successful mixed-traffic steam locomotive ever, the Royal Prussian Union Railway's P8 class originated as a modified version of an unsuccessful express engine produced in 1906. The P8 was adopted by other railways in Germany, and many were supplied to other countries as reparations after World War I. Some Belgian examples worked until the withdrawal of steam in 1966. Production as Class 38 continued in Germany until 1928, reaching a total of 3,438 – plus some 500-odd built in other countries during and after World War II. P8s were used by German forces in Czechoslovakia, Greece, Poland, Romania, the Soviet Union and Yugoslavia, which all retained the type in peacetime and made alterations of their own. Many P8s are preserved, (at least eight in Germany), and others may be in former Soviet Union countries **WHERE TO SEE IT** P8s sometimes appear in Plandampf events (see Class 18 next page) in Germany or Holland, and in 1995 one was maintained at Wolsztyn shed, Poland, for excursions. Keep an eye on Railway Magazine for latest information.

CLASS 18 4-6-2 – GERMANY

◀ *The unique Class 18 No 201.*

TECHNICAL DETAILS
Semi-streamlined and strikingly painted, No 18.201 was built at the Deutsche Reichsbahn experimental establishment at Halle in 1961. Parts from a 4-6-4 tank and a 2-10-2 freight loco were combined with huge 2.3 m (90.5 in) driving wheels. A new boiler, working at 16.2 kg/sq cm (230 psi) fed three cylinders. Maximum speed about 160 km/h (100 mph).

In the early 1990s a new word, 'Plandampf', entered the vocabulary of rail enthusiasts. First German railways, then Dutch, turned regular scheduled trains over to steam haulage for the occasional weekend, and the practice has since spread to South Africa. A Plandampf is typically held in a limited area, but freights, local trains and fast expresses are worked at their usual speeds by superbly maintained vintage steam locos. Many sheds in East Germany retained steam for reserve and heating purposes, and some of these are now regarded as 'museum'

depots. One such is Saalfeld, home of the locomotive shown here, the sole DR Class 18 Pacific, a semi-streamlined experimental express engine built in 1961. This magnificent olive green-painted machine, which often reached 160 km/h (100 mph) in service, has now been one of the stars at several Plandampfs.

WHERE TO SEE IT In late 1995, No 18.201 was based at Saalfeld, a steam museum shed near Jena in eastern Germany and the focus of several Plandampf events in recent years.

ICE – GERMANY

TECHNICAL DETAILS

The 14-car trains of ICE 2 will be similar to the first series, but equipped with nose couplings and a new quick-reacting light-weight pantograph. Trains will carry 394 passengers at up to 280 km/h (174 mph). The Bo-Bo power cars each weigh 78 tonnes and develop 5,000 kW (6,500 hp). The braking system includes electromagnetic skids that act directly on the rails. Unpowered control cars for half-trains are expected by 1998.

German Railways, the Deutsche Bahn Aktiengemeinschaft is building a network of high-speed lines like those of France, Spain and Japan. The Inter City Express (ICE) trains entered service in 1991 between Munich and Hamburg via either Wurzburg or Frankfurt and Stuttgart, and now also run between Hamburg and Zurich via Basle. By 1995 the system was carrying 65,000 passengers on 115 runs daily at up to 280 km/h (174 mph). A new version, ICE 2, is due to enter service in 1996. This can be coupled nose-to-nose, and a special control car is being developed to allow half-length trains to

▲ *Shovel-nose high-speed ICE trains are the pride of Germany's rail system.*

operate with just one power car. An even more advanced third-generation ICE now being planned will be more like the Japanese Shinkansen trains, with two axles in every coach motorised.
WHERE TO SEE IT The ICE trains serve Hamburg, Hanover, Frankfurt, Basle, Zurich, Wurzburg, Munich, Bremen, Stuttgart, Kassel and Berlin. Really high-speed running is limited to the new sections of the Munich-Hamburg line.

GE 6/6 I 'BABY CROC' – SWITZERLAND

Character is something that steam enthusiasts rarely attribute to electric locomotives, but the articulated 'Crocodile', with its overhanging roof, long bonnets and fascinating jackshaft drive motion, is an exception. Standard-gauge crocs, built from 1920 for the Swiss Federal Railways, inspired this smaller version for the metre-gauge Rhaetian Railway, and the name 'Baby Croc' was inevitable, though it was for a while the world's most powerful metre-gauge loco. The Rhaetian Railway serves the ski resorts of Davos, St Moritz and Klosters in southern Switzerland. It has 116 tunnels and 483 bridges in 392 km (244 miles) of track, and has inherited four types of electrification from its constituent lines. The 11,000 volt ac system is to be extended, and regular motive power is state-of-the-art, but steam and vintage electric locos are also retained for tourist and enthusiast specials.

WHERE TO SEE IT On the main lines of the Rhaetian Railway (Rhaetische Bahn) in the Swiss Canton of Graubunden. Two or three out of the five surviving Baby Crocs are presently available to haul regular excursions as well as the occasional freight.

▲ *Baby Croc No E402 waiting at Tiefencastel, Switzerland.*

TECHNICAL DETAILS
Rh B Class Ge 6/6I, built by SLM and Brown Boveri, 1921-1929. Wheel arrangement C-C. Power supply 11 kV ac overhead. Weight 66 tonnes. Maximum speed 55 km/h (34 mph). Length 13.3 m (43 ft 8 in). Articulated body.

BRB RACK RAILWAY – SWITZERLAND

◄ *One of the Brienz-Rothorn Bahn's original steam locomotives pushes its coach up the steep rack section.*

TECHNICAL DETAILS

In classic-design European rack locos, two cylinders drive a shaft mounted amidships. This shaft carries the large pinion wheel which engages the rack between the rails; cranks on the shaft's ends are coupled to the wheels. The new Waller design is much the same, but burns diesel oil, and has automatic boiler management and overnight electric water heating – this excellent feature allows a Waller loco to be ready to go within 15 minutes of the driver arriving.

The oldest rack railway in Switzerland's Bernese Oberland is the Brienz-Rothorn Bahn (BRB), which was opened in 1892 to link the lakeside town of Brienz with a hotel near the summit of the Brienzer Rothorn mountain. The 7.6 km line rises 1,682 m (5,515 ft) at gradients up to 25 per cent, the greatest altitude gain of any Swiss rack railway. Until fairly recently, the BRB was the only Swiss line operated entirely by steam, with a stop for water at the half-way station at Planalp. The picture above shows one such BRB steam loco. Diesels eventually took over except for the occasional steam 'special', but steam did

return in 1992 and in revolutionary form at that – an oil-fired loco from the SLM works, based at Winterthur. The brainchild of Swiss engineer Roger Waller, the design is clean and quiet in operation, at least as efficient as a diesel, and can be operated by just one person.

WHERE TO SEE IT Brienz is not far from Interlaken, at the east end of this beautiful lake. For the energetic, the summit of the Rothorn at 2,353 m (7,717 ft) can be reached on foot from Bruenig-Hasliberg on the Interlaken-Lucerne line. The BRB itself is open from June to September.

KRAUSS 0-6-2T – AUSTRIA

▶ *The immaculate 0-6-2T No 3 of the Zillertal Railway prepares for work.*

Austria still has a number of narrow-gauge railways (both state-owned and private) and some of them still use steam power, at least during the summer tourist season. The Krauss U-class 0-6-2 tank shown here is a standard model on the 760 mm (30 in) gauge lines. Jenbach in the Tyrol is a terminus to two such railways, the Achensee rack line and the Zillertalbahn (Ziller Valley Railway) to Mayrhofen. The Ziller, a working line which carries local passengers as well as standard-gauge freight wagons perched on top of special narrow-gauge trucks, is privately owned. With help from summer volunteers (including some Brits!) it manages to break even, and is a valuable tourist asset to the area. Its steam fleet, consisting of 0-6-2 tanks and a single 0-10-0, is limited to summer passenger traffic – diesels handle everything else.

WHERE TO SEE IT Jenbach is east of Innsbruck on the main line to Munich, and on the A12 Autobahn. The Zillertalbahn follows the road to Mayrhofen, a popular holiday resort in the Tyrolean Alps.

TECHNICAL DETAILS

The picture shows a Zillertalbahn Krauss U-class 0-6-2 tank. This early engine has slide valves in inclined steam chests; later versions have piston valves, which allow steam to expand more fully in the cylinders before being exhausted. The state-owned Murtal railway, from Unzmarkt to Mautendorf, also uses engines of this class.

ETR 450 – ITALY

▶ *The ETR 450 Pendolino leans into curves for a more comfortable ride at speed.*

TECHNICAL DETAILS

The Fiat Ferroviaria ETR 450 went into service in 1988. Each train has eight B-B power cars and one trailer. Two motors in each car drive wheels via jointed shafts and bevel gears. Power supply is 3,000 volt dc overhead. Overall train length 183.6 m (602 ft 4 in), total weight 400 tonnes. Maximum speed 250 km/h (155 mph).

One of several tilting-body expresses now in operation around the world, the Italian ETR (Elettrotreno Rapido) 450 'Pendolino' links Rome and Milan, 600 km (372 miles) in just under four hours, at speeds up to 250 km/h (155 mph). The nine-car trains, with all cars powered except one, also run between Milan and Turin, Rome and Naples, and Rome and Venice. By leaning into curves like a cyclist, the train can take them at higher speed for less passenger discomfort than can a conventional train. Car bodies are tilted by hydraulic rams, con-trolled by a computer that reacts to motion sensors. The Fiat-designed chassisless car bodies are built of light alloy. Like the abortive British APT of the early 1980s, Pendolino's body is mounted on converging pivoted struts above the bogies – however, this system works reliably, unlike that of the APT. The newer and faster, but non-tilting ETR 500 is now in service on more straight-and-level routes.

WHERE TO SEE IT On main lines between Rome, Milan, Turin and Venice.

AVE – SPAIN

◀ *Spain's AVE has slightly softened TGV contours.*

TECHNICAL DETAILS

AVE is a ten-car train, built by GEC Alsthom in France. Two Bo-Bo power cars produce 8,000 kW (10,720 hp). Power supply 25 kV ac overhead on high-speed line, 3 kV overhead in Madrid and Seville areas. Overall length just over 200 m (657 ft), weight 421.5 tonnes. Passenger capacity 329 in three classes. Maximum speed, 300 km/h (186 mph).

For its new 471 km (292.5 mile) high-speed line between Madrid and Seville, RENFE (Spanish National Railways) chose a restyled version of the French TGV, named the Alta Velocidad Espanola (Spanish High Speed). The trains, mechanically almost identical to the TGV-A but with eight coaches instead of ten, have dual-voltage electrics for 25,000 and 3,000 volt supplies, while passengers have more legroom and individual audio facilities. To cope with Spain's sunny climate, air-conditioning and brake-cooling systems have been uprated. Six of the 24 trains ordered will have temporary axles of Spanish wide gauge – 1.67 m (65.75 in) – for the Barcelona to Valencia line. The Spanish system also includes German-made Class 252 locos to haul freight and dual-gauge Talgo express trains on the new line at up to 220 km/h (136 mph). Present speed limits are 270 km/h (168 mph) for AVE and 200 km/h (125 mph) for loco-hauled Talgo stock.

WHERE TO SEE IT Between Madrid-Atocha and Seville Santa Justa, via Ciudad Real, Puertollano and Cordoba.

CLASS 242 4-8-4 – SPAIN

TECHNICAL DETAILS

The Class 242 had two cylinders with poppet valves driven by Walschaert gear. Driving wheels were 1.9 m (75 in) in diameter. 242s were built as oil burners, with a capacity of 13,500 litres of oil (3,000 galls) and a water capacity of 28,000 litres (6,200 galls). Weight 213 tonnes. Length overall 26.84 m (88 ft 1 in). Roller bearings fitted on all axles.

A dozen of this 4-8-4 steam engine class were built in 1955 by Maquinista Terrestre y Maritima of Barcelona to haul expresses on the non-electrified part of the line from Madrid to the French border. To fit available turntables, the engines had very short tenders for their size, and this seriously limited their non-stop range. Performance was superb, though with a speed limit of 110 km/h (68 mph) their maximum speed of 130 km-plus was academic. The 242s handled 750-tonne expresses with ease even on steeply-graded lines. Very well equipped, locomotives had a sprung cab floor to absorb vibration, a turbo-generator for train lighting, and even a light shining on the chimney to show the fireman the colour of the exhaust at night!

WHERE TO SEE IT 242 No 2009 is preserved by RENFE at Miranda del Ebro, though at present, a tendency to derail keeps it off the main line. Alignment errors may have been made during maintenance.

▲ *242 No 2010 photographed near Pancorbo, Spain.*

RAIL: THE WORLD CHANGER

The coming of the railways had many unexpected side-effects

▲ *Postal services were a beneficiary of the rail revolution, with on-board sorting facilities a major plus.*

Rail travel as we know it – metal wheels on metal rails – is coming up for its 200th anniversary. In less than a decade it will be two centuries since Cornish engineer Richard Trevithick's first steam locomotive went into action at the Pen-y-Darren ironworks in South Wales. The changes in locomotive design have been well-documented, and much of this book is dedicated to showing a cross-section of that development, from *Rocket* to TGV. What is less well known are some of the side-effects that the rail explosion had, both on people's lives and in spurring technological progress.

A GOLDEN AGE OF RAIL

The 19th century was the golden age of rail – railways were spreading all around the world, steel tentacles extending between cities and into the country. Some of the changes brought about by these new links (and in the 1800s, rail was the cutting-edge technology of the day) were dramatic. For instance, before the railways, you could buy a loaf of bread in the south of France, where wheat was grown, for a quarter the price in Paris. The extra 300 per cent on a loaf represented the costs involved in a three-day horse-drawn journey to the capital, plus spoilage and losses on the way. With the advent of the railway, these costs were dramatically cut and food in cities soon cost little more than where it had been grown. In Switzerland, the first railway was nicknamed the 'bread train', as it brought fresh-made rolls to the burghers of Zurich each morning, the first time that you could guarantee that the ingredients had not been stored several days. Farm-fresh foods of all sorts became common for the first time in cities – milk, fruit, vegetables, meat, fish – none had been available before on a regular basis.

◀ *Rail travel in the 19th century often meant excitement and adventure – trips to exotic destinations were possible, and if you could pay the extra, then comfortable sleepers and fine food in restaurant cars were available at a premium.*

FAMOUS NAMES

Two centuries of rail travel has left a legacy of successful and not-so-successful companies and organisations. Some of this long list of famous names, badges, logos and symbols are shown on the right.

Great Western Railway (left), known to supporters as 'God's Wonderful Railway'. American company Santa Fe's colourful logo (above). The Canadian Pacific used a beaver (right).

BRINGING BACK THE ICE

A by-product of the growth in food transportation (and essential for taking perishable goods over long distances by train) was the ice industry, which by the mid-19th century was a massive business. Insulated ice stores were filled in winter by hacking out frozen lakes. In places where there was no winter ice (in California, for example) teams were sent into the Sierras and Rockies to bring back supplies from mountain peaks and glaciers. Important as it was, the ice industry went into rapid decline after refrigeration equipment was developed in the latter half of the 19th century.

The rail explosion drove other areas of technology to new heights, not least the design and construction of bridges and tunnels, often using new materials and pioneering structural methods that were the leading edge of the day. Engineers like Brunel were building structures unlike anything required before, though construction techniques themselves often remained primitive in the extreme. For the 3,000 m (9,840 ft)

Box Tunnel near Bath, a workforce of some 4,000 people was required, with 300 horses used to carry out the waste. Each week the tunnel diggers got through a tonne of candles for light and a tonne of gunpowder for rock blasting. Some structures remain unequalled right up to this day – for example, the 1889 Forth Bridge still stands as the most massive steel rail bridge ever built.

DAWN OF THE TOURIST INDUSTRY

Perhaps the greatest social change wrought by the railways was the new-found ability to travel, easily, quickly and relatively cheaply. Before the railways, few people had the time or the money to venture far from where they lived. Now rail travel and the excitement of exploring new places became a popular game. First it was only for the rich, but then, with the advent of the first 'packages' tailored for greater numbers of travellers (they were pioneered by Thomas Cook and Co, a firm that is still successfully in the travel business), the not-so-rich could join in the fun, too. The age of the tourist had dawned!

▲ *The rail bridge over the Firth of Forth, Scotland, here used by a Class 47 diesel and train. The bridge is still in constant use and remains the largest of its kind in the world. Despite the more recent suspension bridge, this one is 'the' Forth Bridge, so far as most people are concerned!*

Heraldic lion of British Railways (above), Chesapeake &.Ohio pussy cat (above right) and Union Pacific shield (right).

Letters in wheels for the Trans Europe Express (above) and a simple oval for Belgium's Railways (right).

BRITISH ISLES

Britain produced the first steam railway locomotive, by Richard Trevithick in 1804, the first public steam railway in 1825, and the first inter-city line in 1830. By the turn of the century, there was a network covering the country. World wars affected the railways seriously, with 120 companies amalgamating into four in 1923, then being nationalised in 1948. Closures of branch lines in the 1960s cut the network almost by half, and government policy favoured roads; however main line electrification was extended, and some rolling stock modernised. There was little investment in the early 1980s though: track, signals and rolling stock deteriorated and no high-speed lines were built. Road congestion and the Channel Tunnel have revived some official interest, but Britain is now behind much of Europe. Ireland's railways have followed similar lines, leaving a reduced system, but one that is being modernised and, in an improving social and economic climate, having a hopeful future. Meanwhile on the enthusiast front, over 1,000 standard-gauge steam locomotives have been preserved, and for the tourist and rail fan, the romance of the rails is still big business.

Picture above shows an SR Class S15 in action.

'ROCKET' 0-2-2

▶ *The National Railway Museum's replica.*

The world's first inter-city railway, the Liverpool and Manchester, held a competition at Rainhill in October 1829 to select the best locomotive for its projected service. Of three serious contenders, the winner was the *Rocket*, built by George Stephenson and his son Robert at their Newcastle works. It had three features seen in nearly all steam locos since – multi-tube boiler; narrowed blast pipe to accelerate exhaust steam up the chimney, drawing the fire to suit the amount of steam being used; and driving cranks set at 90 degrees to each other for smooth thrust transmission to the wheels. *Rocket*'s high-mounted cylinders were lowered to reduce oscillation, but the engine remained unstable. It was soon outmoded and ended working life as a colliery engine, but a big place in rail history as the first practical passenger locomotive was assured.
WHERE TO SEE IT The original engine, much rebuilt, is in the Science Museum, London. Of several replicas, the best was completed in 1979 for the National Railway Museum, York. This engine is occasionally steamed, and has also attended various events abroad.

TECHNICAL DETAILS
Weight 4.1 tonnes. Driving wheels 1.42 m (56 in) in diameter. Steam pressure 4.2 kg/sq cm (60 psi) and primitive all-or-nothing valve gear fitted. Initially, *Rocket* had no brakes – to stop, the driver juggled valve levers to put the engine into reverse.

CLASS A3 4-6-2 'FLYING SCOTSMAN'

▶ Flying Scotsman *finished in 1962 BR livery, complete with smoke deflectors and double chimney.*

TECHNICAL DETAILS
4-6-2 Pacific, with driving wheels 2.03 m (80 in) in diameter. Three cylinders. Gresley 'conjugated' valve gear drives middle cylinder valves via a transverse beam. Steam pressure 15.75 kg/sq cm (225 psi). Double chimney, fitted in the early 1960s enhances steam generation. Length 21.46 m (70 ft 5 in).

Sir Nigel Gresley's three-cylinder 4-6-2 express locomotives for the LNER originated as the A1 class of 1922. Seventy-nine of the type were built, all but one of them later running as BR A3s, with higher-pressure boilers. Capable of 100 mph running (though this was seldom required), some of these Pacifics received corridor tenders to allow exchange of crews while working non-stop expresses over the 632 km (392 miles) London-Edinburgh route. A speed of 174 km/h (108 mph) was reached with a test train for the 'Silver Jubilee' express in 1935, and this stands as a record for non-streamlined locos. Only one A3, the world-famous No 4472 *Flying*

Scotsman, survives. At present this loco is in its 1960s BR colour scheme and number. The 'blinkers' at the front were added to the unadorned original to deflect smoke away from the cab. Opinions as to whether the looks of the big loco are improved are divided!

WHERE TO SEE IT In 1995, *Flying Scotsman* began a major overhaul, involving heavy boiler repairs, for a renewal of its main-line operating certificate. It should eventually reappear, as BR No 60103 with double chimney and smoke deflectors, as worn over the 1994-95 seasons. For information, telephone Waterman Railways 01543 419472/254076.

CLASS A4 4-6-2

eveloped in 1935 in just six months for the LNER's 'Silver Jubilee' express between London and Newcastle, the three-cylinder A4 proved able to haul the heaviest expresses and even freight trains. The first of the new locos, built to maintain a four-hour schedule on the run, was *Silver Link*, which hit a top speed of just over 181 km/h (112.5 mph) in September 1935 trials. To go with the new locomotives, the 'Silver Jubilee' express was provided with specially-built silver-grey streamlined stock. Thirty-five of the good-looking A4 streamliners were built, the last seven being fitted with French-design Kylchap double chimneys. On 3 July 1938, the first of these double-chimney A4s, No 4468 *Mallard*, set what has proved to be the all-time official speed record for steam. Hauling a seven-coach brake-testing train on Stoke Bank between Grantham and Peterborough it touched 202.8 km/h (126 mph). The nearest rival to this record is the German Borsig 05 001, which hit 200.4 km/h (124.5 mph) three years before.

WHERE TO SEE IT Six A4s have been preserved, including one at Green Bay, Wisconsin, USA, and one at Delson, Quebec, Canada. *Mallard* is on display at the National Railway Museum, York (Tel: 01904 621261). A4s *Sir Nigel Gresley* and *Union of South Africa* appear frequently on main-line excursions. *Bittern*, painted as *Silver Link*, is under restoration at the Great Central Railway, Loughborough.

TECHNICAL DETAILS
The A4 4-6-2 has an axle load of 22.5 tonnes and a total weight of 170 tonnes. Steam pressure is 17.5 kg/sq cm (250 psi), and driving wheel diameter is 2.32 m (80 in). Overall length is 21.65 m (71 ft).

▲ *No 4468* Mallard, *the world speed-record holder for steam. The engine hauled various specials in the 1980s, but is now at the National Railway Museum, York, and no further outings are expected.*

▼ *Two A4s undergo maintenance work in a locomotive shed.*

CLASS C 0-6-0

▶ *Gleaming paint-work and carefully applied lining mark out* Maude *as being in an immaculate state of preservation.*

TECHNICAL DETAILS
North British Railway Class C, BR Class J36. Goods engine of 0-6-0 tender type used in great numbers up to the 1930s. Class C locos have two inside cylinders, 1.52 m (60 in) driving wheels, boiler working at 11.55 kg/sq cm (165 psi). Weight in working order 76.9 tonnes.

North British Railway No 673 *Maude* is the sole survivor of 168 Class C 0-6-0 goods engines built between 1888 and 1900. Its name commemorates a British commander, General Maude, and was acquired following service on the Western Front during World War I. In recent years, this loco (based on the Bo'ness and Kinneil Railway in Scotland) has performed on main line excursions, and travelled to the 150th anniversary celebrations of the Liverpool and Manchester Railway under its own steam in 1980. Designed by Matthew Holmes, the class received the distinctive side-window cab intro-

duced by WP Reid in the Edwardian period. All Class C locos were taken over by the LNER in the 'grouping' of 1923, when no less than 120 railway companies were merged to form just four. After this Class C was renamed J36, and 86 of them worked on the Scottish Region of British Railways before the mass scrapping of steam in the 1960s.

WHERE TO SEE IT The 5.6 km (3.5 miles) Bo'ness and Kinneil Railway is on the south shore of the Firth of Forth, near Edinburgh. It is open every weekend, and daily in the summer season. For details, contact 01506 822298.

CLASS 0415 ADAMS 4-4-2T

William Adams was first the Locomotive Superintendent of the North London Railway, then of the London and South Western Railway (LSWR). Besides the superb passenger 4-4-0s he designed for the LSWR, he was responsible for the distinctive and long-lived 4-4-2 tank class for local passenger services shown here, the first one of which ran in 1882. Their rear axles, mounted in laterally-sliding bearings, gave these engines the unofficial title of 'Adams Radials'. The sole survivor of 71 built is lovingly preserved on the Bluebell Railway, Sussex. Other Adams developments included the invention of a world-standard locomotive bogie, the pivot pin of which was free to slide sideways in a slot so as to follow curves without throwing the driving wheels out of line.

WHERE TO SEE IT With other engines from the former Southern and Great Western Railways, the Adams Radial can be seen on the Bluebell Line in Sussex, which runs between Sheffield Park and Kingscote. The engine's 1901 boiler has been condemned as unsafe, but someday the loco will be restored to running order. Meanwhile, visitors can see it on static display at Sheffield Park. For information, telephone 01825 723777.

▲ *Adams Radial gleaming in the bright green livery of the LSWR.*

TECHNICAL DETAILS
Adams 0415-class 4-4-2T locomotives were built by outside contractors from 1882. No 488 shown here weighs just over 55 tonnes and the driving wheel diameter is 1.7 m (67 in). Steam pressure 11.55 kg/sq cm (165 psi)

CLASS 08 SHUNTER

▶ *08 shunters can be seen almost anywhere on the rail system. This one is shown at Old Oak Common depot, West London.*

Britain's most prolific locomotive class ever, the BR standard diesel shunter is based on a design introduced in the 1930s by the LMS. From 1953, 1,193 of this type (including the rarer Class 09 version) were built, and they can still be seen on shunting duty in yards and stations. Several have now been preserved, even on steam railways, which use them for track maintenance work and for shunting when passenger numbers do not justify steaming an extra loco. Diesel fans, of course, need no excuses! As more of these shunters come into private hands, new liveries are appearing, and many have been painted in older BR colours, or even in variations on pre-nationalisation schemes. English Electric built 125 shunters for export to Holland, where many are still at work.

WHERE TO SEE IT In mainland Britain, you are rarely far from an 08 shunter. With a top speed of just 32 km/h (20 mph, 27 mph for the class 09) they seldom go on main lines, but most motive power depots have at least one. Preserved examples are at Didcot Railway Centre (tel: 01235 817200), Quainton Road, Bucks (tel: 01296 655450), and Llangollen, Clwyd (tel: 01978 860979), to name just three places.

CLASS 7MT 4-6-2

TECHNICAL DETAILS

Class 7MT 4-6-2. Like many American locomotives, 'Brits' have just two cylinders and a high running board, leaving wheels and motion completely exposed to view. The cab is attached directly to the firebox rather than to the frames. Driving wheels are 1.88 m (74 in) diameter and steam pressure is 17.5 kg/sq cm (250 psi). The loco weighs 141.2 or 149.5 tonnes, depending on the type of tender attached.

Following the formation of British Railways on 1 January 1948 by the amalgamation of the 'Big Four' companies – GWR, LMS, LNER and SR – several new classes of steam locomotive were ordered. These were to be standardised throughout the new system, combining the best features of Big Four designs, with accessible working parts for ease of maintenance. Flagship of the series and unveiled at the Festival of Britain exhibition of 1951, was the fast mixed traffic Class 7MT, painted in green passenger livery and having a mellow-toned chime whistle. Locomotive No 70000 *Britannia* gave its name unofficially to

CLASS 9F 2-10-0

▶ *Class 9F loco* Black Prince *on a run in Lancashire, April 1995.*

British steam made its farewell with this, the most successful of the 12 standard classes produced for the BR system. Nicknamed 'spaceships' for their rocket-like high-mounted boilers, locos of this 251-strong class could pull heavy freights with ease, and, despite their small driving wheels, sometimes handled fast passenger trains. One exceeded 145 km/h (90 mph) with an Eastern Region express! No 92220, the last steam loco built for British Railways, was named

Evening Star and emerged from Swindon works in 1960, in full passenger livery with a GWR-style copper-capped chimney. Sadly, the average lifespan of these engines was only ten years.

WHERE TO SEE IT Working 9Fs can be seen in various places, including the East Somerset Railway at Cranmore, and the Bluebell Railway, Sussex. Six more locos are in various states of restoration around the UK. *Evening Star* is at the National Railway Museum, York.

TECHNICAL DETAILS

Locomotives of the 2-10-0 9F class have relatively small driving wheels, just 1.52 m (60 in) in diameter. Steam pressure is 17.5 kg/sq cm (250 psi). Tender load is just over 9 tonnes of coal, with 21,480 litres (4,725 galls) of water. Total weight 142.19 tonnes.

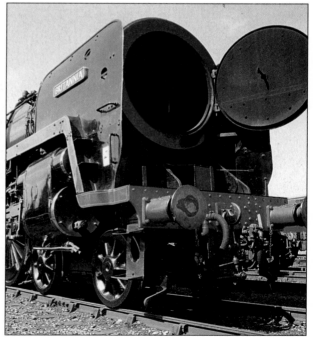

◀ *British Railways Class 7MT No 70000* Britannia; *picture taken at the Didcot Railway Centre, August 1995.*

▼ *The same loco, smokebox door hanging open – pure delight for the lover of classic British steam!*

the entire class of 55 engines, all built in Crewe and completed by 1954. After a few teething troubles, the 'Brits' distinguished themselves by hauling expresses on the Eastern and Southern regions, and eventually most of the UK. All the Britannias were withdrawn by 1968 during BR's hasty dieselisation programme. There are just two survivors, *Britannia* and *Oliver Cromwell*.

WHERE TO SEE IT No 70013 *Oliver Cromwell* is on static display at Bressingham Steam Museum, Norfolk. No 70000 *Britannia* will be operating at various locations during 1996, returning to Didcot from time to time.

CLASS 57XX PANNIER TANK

Britain's most numerous steam loco class, no less than 863 '57's were built from 1929 to 1950. Even so, they were just one of several pannier or 'matchbox' tank classes used by the Great Western Railway from the turn of the century to the end of steam in the 1960s. Earlier examples were mostly rebuilds of old saddle tanks, but the 57xx was based on the Dean Goods tender locomotive of 1883. Pannier tanks shunted, hauled local freight and passenger trains, and operated push-pull 'auto trains', either from the middle or from one end with a cab-equipped coach at the other. Some 57s worked on the Southern Region, notably at Folkestone, and others were fitted with condensing apparatus to recycle exhaust steam into the tanks on the London Underground.

WHERE TO SEE IT On many preserved railways, as far north as the Keighley and Worth Valley in Yorkshire. The Buckinghamshire Railway Centre's No 7715 (in London Transport livery as L99) runs annually on the outer suburban part of the Metropolitan Line. The Bucks Centre is based at Quainton, near Aylesbury. Telephone 01296 655450.

▲▼ *This immaculately-restored 57xx can be admired, and seen in action from time to time, at the excellent Didcot Railway Centre in Oxfordshire.*

TECHNICAL DETAILS
Class 57xx 0-6-0PT. There are several number series and variations in fittings and cab style among the 16 remaining engines, but all have 1.41 m (55.5 in) driving wheels and two cylinders. They weigh about 50 tonnes, are 9.5 m (31 ft 2in) long. Working steam pressure is 140 kg/sq cm (200 psi).

CLASS 43 HST

◀ HST express at full speed.

TECHNICAL DETAILS
Each power car has a Paxman Valenta or Mirrlees MB190 12-cylinder diesel engine of 1,680 kw (2,250 hp). Transmission is via a Brush alternator to Brush or GEC traction motors, with a Bo-Bo wheel arrangement. Maximum speed 201 km/h (125 mph) in service, but higher speeds have been attained on test. The usual HST train consists of eight Mk 3 coaches and two power cars.

The distinctive 'whizz-whoosh-whizz' sound of the good-looking High Speed Train was first heard on the Western Region of British Rail in 1976. At a stroke, speeds increased from 160 km/h (100 mph) to 201 km/h (125 mph), yet passengers were able to enjoy a quieter, smoother ride than they had on any previous British train. HSTs next replaced Deltic-hauled trains on the fast East Coast main line, later to be replaced in turn by electric haulage. They now mainly operate Great Western, Midland Main Line and CrossCountry services. HST power units are worked in pairs at either end of a train, and more than 190 of them (now designated Class 43) were built at Crewe by British Rail Engineering.

WHERE TO SEE IT Mainly on Great Western and Midland lines from Paddington and St Pancras stations, London. Increasingly however, they can be seen operating on other through-routes such as London Euston to Holyhead.

CLASS 91 INTERCITY 225

Introduced in 1988, these locomotives were designed for the newly-electrified East Coast main line between King's Cross and Edinburgh, running under the 'Intercity 225' banner. When resignalling is completed on this line, the sleek 91s will be able to haul regular trains at up to 225 km/h (140 mph), hence the name. Already however, higher speeds have been achieved – on 2 June 1995, a six-coach train powered by Class 91 No 91031 *Sir Henry Royce* achieved a British record of 248 km/h (154 mph) between Grantham and Peterborough. Trains powered by these locos have a driving van trailer at the far end, so they can be driven in either direction. The asymmetric loco design has one cab end streamlined, the other flat. The 91 can also work with a modified HST power car at the other end of the train, allowing it to operate on non-electrified lines.

WHERE TO SEE IT On the East Coast main line. The termini at London King's Cross, Edinburgh Waverley and Leeds are the best vantage points. Doncaster, Grantham and Peterborough are good places between.

▲ An InterCity 225, headed by Class 91 No 91001, travels north at speed.

TECHNICAL DETAILS

Built from 1988-91 by BREL at Crewe. Power supply 25 kV ac overhead. Maximum rail power 4,700 kW (6,300 hp) from GEC G 426AZ traction motors in Bo-Bo arrangement. Maximum service speed 225 km/h (140 mph). Length 19.4 m (63 ft 8 in). Weight 84 tonnes.

CLASS 92

▶ *Class 92 loco No 92030 De Falla emerging from the Channel Tunnel, June 1995. Note the distinctive triple-tunnel logo behind the cab.*

To haul freight and sleeping car trains through the Channel Tunnel, a new class of electric locomotive is being built by Brush Traction of Loughborough. The 46 Class 92 engines are divided into 30 for UK freight, seven for UK passenger service and a further nine for SNCF. Between London and the Tunnel, the locos use third-rail pickup, with a pantograph available for overhead supply. In the Tunnel itself, a pair of 92s work each train, one either end as insurance against breakdown. As freight and sleeper speeds in the UK are not very high, the locos (named mostly after authors and composers) are

geared for pulling power rather than outright speed. The two-tone green overnight passenger coaches are also in production at the time of writing, and will connect various cities in the UK with continental destinations such as Paris, Brussels, Amsterdam, Dortmund and Frankfurt.

WHERE TO SEE IT On freight, between Willesden Freight Depot, London, Folkestone and the Calais Freight Depot. All are based at Crewe. Class 92s will haul overnight passenger services from Glasgow, London Olympia or Waterloo.

TECHNICAL DETAILS

Co-Co class 92 built by Brush Traction at Loughborough, with electrical equipment by ABB, Zurich. The dual-supply system consists of 25kV ac overhead and 750 volts dc third-rail. Brush-built traction motors give a continuous output of 5,000 kW (6,700 hp) and a maximum speed of 140 km/h (87.5 mph). Overall length 21.34 m (70 ft). Cab signalling equipment is installed for use in the Channel Tunnel.

CLASS 165

▲ *Chiltern Turbos from London Marylebone use Class 165/0 units. This one is near Haddenham, in Aylesbury Vale, July 1995.*

Since the 1950s, the UK rail system has used diesel multiple-unit (DMU) trains for stopping and commuter traffic on non-electrified lines. A lengthy period of low investment during the 1970s and 1980s saw elderly DMUs run almost into the ground, but since then, the construction of new designs, notably Sprinters, Super Sprinters and Turbos, has brought a welcome update to the fleet. The remaining old-style DMUs are now known as 'Heritage' units, a piece of official wool-over-the-eyes, if ever there was one. The Class 165/0 turbo-diesel-hydraulic stock shown here was built in 1990-1992 for local services from Marylebone on the Chiltern line. All cars in each set of two or three are powered, and sets can be coupled together to make a train of any length required. For passengers, a relatively small BR investment in Marylebone Station has worked wonders. It now has good facilities, including a comfortable deli-style shopping zone.

TECHNICAL DETAILS

The Class 165/0 was built by BREL Ltd. There is one 260 kw (350 hp) Perkins 2006-TWH engine in each car, with hydraulic transmission. Each car is 23.5 m (77 ft 1 in) long, and weighs 37 tonnes. Top speed is 120 km/h (75 mph). The 165/1 and 166 classes are somewhat faster, with a maximum speed of 145 km/h (90 mph).

WHERE TO SEE IT On suburban lines out of London Marylebone. The very similar Class 165/1 operates from Paddington up the Thames line, and as far afield as Worcester and Birmingham. An air-conditioned variant, the Class 166, runs between Paddington and Oxford.

EUROTUNNEL SHUTTLE LOCOMOTIVE

▲ *Le Shuttle locos are not as sleek as their Eurostar siblings, but they do provide a reliable point-to-point service through the tunnel.*

TECHNICAL DETAILS

Shuttle locos have a Bo-Bo-Bo wheel arrangement. Each loco has six ASEA Brown Boveri 3-phase traction motors totalling 5,600 kW from a supply system operating at 25 kV, 50 Hz ac. Maximum speed is 160 km/h (100 mph), though in-tunnel speeds are not so high. In order to accommodate big loads such as container trucks, coaches and caravans, the rolling stock has a special loading gauge of 4.1 m wide and up to 5.6 m high.

The tallest and widest trains in the world have been built for the vehicle-carrying Shuttle service through the Channel Tunnel. Over 800 metres long and weighing 2,400 tonnes, these trains require powerful locomotives that can push and pull them up tunnel exit gradients of 1 in 90. The Euroshuttle Locomotive Consortium built 38 of these Shuttle units at Loughborough during 1992-94. All locos are named after opera singers, and they perform 'duets', one engine at either end of a train. For the most compact power package possible, locos have three powered bogies, and state-of-the-art electronics give ultra-smooth motor control throughout the speed range. Because of their size – a truck-carrier Shuttle could accommodate a complete TGV train and track, without it

even touching sides or ceiling – these vehicles can operate only on the loop track of the Eurotunnel system. A few months after opening, Eurotunnel was already claiming over half the cross-Channel market for trucks. A new user may be the British Army, which is keen to move its tanks to and from European exercise areas by train, reducing road congestion and earning it 'green' points with environmental groups.

WHERE TO SEE IT The Channel Tunnel runs between two terminals, Folkestone, Kent and Coquelles, near Calais, France. Passengers get a close look at the locomotives, though it is rather brief, just while loading and unloading. For booking information, contact Customer Service on 0990 35 35 35.

CLASS 201 – IRELAND

► One of Irish Rail's Class 201 express locos at Mallow, on the Dublin-Cork line.

TECHNICAL DETAILS
General Motors EMD Class 201 Co-Co diesel-electric, type JT42 HCW, built in GM's Ontario works. The single engine is a GM 12-710 G3B twelve-cylinder two-stroke diesel rated at 2,380 kW (3,200 hp). Total weight is 113 tonnes, maximum speed 161 km/h (100 mph).

Ireland's railways have always been a bit special, from their main-line gauge of 160 cm (63 in) to the extraordinary Lartigue-design Listowel and Ballybunion steam monorail in County Kerry, which closed in 1924. Today the network is trimmed down to main and commuter lines, and Iarnrod Eireann (Irish Rail) is busily modernising its locos and rolling stock. Air-conditioned expresses are now comprehensively equipped, some even having telephones and fax machines on board. Delivery of the 32-strong diesel-electric Class 201 from the North American General Motors company was completed in 1995, and these have now taken over long-distance passenger services except on the Dublin to Rosslare, Sligo and Waterford lines, for which they are too heavy. The first loco to arrive, No 201, was actually *flown* to Ireland in the belly of a giant Russian Antonov 124 jet freighter! In a more traditional vein, steam excursions run regularly between Dublin and Rosslare.

WHERE TO SEE IT Class 201 diesels run on main lines throughout much of the Irish Republic. Information from Irish Rail, telephone 00353 1 8363333.

DELTIC

The prototype of one of Britain's most important diesel classes was tested on London-Liverpool and London-Leeds expresses from 1955. A pair of Napier's unusual two-stroke 'Deltic' engines, each with 18 pistons in an inverted triangle (or delta-shape, hence the name) arrangement, gave the new locomotive an enormous power output and a quite distinctive roar. The first of 22 production Deltics appeared in 1961, and the class took over Eastern Region's top expresses out of London King's Cross, improving on the timings of even the best steam locomotives. They were ousted by HST units in the late 1970s, but six have been preserved, as well as the tastily-striped cream-on-blue prototype. During an in-service life of some 20 years, each loco covered in the region of five million km – that's nearly 6,500 km (4,000 miles) every week! Deltics appear occasionally on preserved lines.

WHERE TO SEE IT The prototype Deltic is in the Science Museum, London. Other preserved Deltics are usually to be found at Old Oak Common depot, West London (no public access), the National Railway Museum, North Yorkshire Moors Railway, Great Central at Loughborough, and the Midland Railway Trust, Butterley.

TECHNICAL DETAILS
Deltic Co-Co diesels have Napier engines, each with three crankshafts at the corners of a triangle (or Greek delta). The cylinders form the sides of the triangle, and each ignition stroke pushes two pistons apart. The 3,300 hp from the two engines drives generators which supply power to the traction motors. Design top speed is over 160 km/h (100 mph).

▲ When it was launched the Deltic was the most powerful self-contained diesel-electric loco in the world.

DUCHESS CLASS 4-6-2

▶ *Duchess of Hamilton, shown here reversing to shed yard at Loughborough.*

TECHNICAL DETAILS
Duchess class Pacific, with driving wheels 2.06 m (81 in) in diameter. The boiler's efficiency is boosted by a high degree of superheating, there are four cylinders and steam pressure is 17.6 kg/sq cm (250 psi). Total weight is 164 tonnes and length 22.51 m (73 ft 10 in).

LMS designer Sir William Stanier's masterpiece originated in 1937 as a streamlined and enlarged development of the Princess Royal class to haul the 'Coronation Scot' express between London and Glasgow. On a special run for the newspapers this train set a short-lived British speed record of 182 km/h (114 mph) near Crewe – it entered the station limits at nearly 100 km/h (60 mph) and narrowly avoided derailment! Many of the 38 Duchess locos were streamlined, but the casings were removed between 1945 and 1949. In 1939, No 6234 *Duchess of Abercorn*, with two firemen aboard, recorded the highest power output ever achieved by a British steam loco while climbing Beattock Bank in Scotland at 102 km/h (63 mph).

WHERE TO SEE IT Three Duchess locos survive – *Duchess of Sutherland* is at Bressingham, Norfolk; *City of Birmingham* is in Birmingham Science Museum; *Duchess of Hamilton* is owned by the National Railway Museum and currently operates main line excursions.

KING CLASS 4-6-0

Designer Charles Collett's four-cylinder 4-6-0 'Castle' of 1923 for the Great Western Region was Britain's most powerful passenger locomotive design until the Southern Railway's 4-6-0 'Lord Nelson' class appeared three years later. Rising to the challenge, and needing something more powerful to handle heavy expresses over the steep hills of Devon, Collett designed an enlarged Castle, the mighty 'King' of 1927. Thirty of these green giants were built; they were too heavy to cross the Royal Albert Bridge into Cornwall, but they hauled many GWR prestige expresses on the trunk route to Plymouth, and north to Wolverhampton. Double chimneys were added in the 1950s, and these helped contribute to a class record of 175 km/h (108.5 mph) by No 6015 *King Richard III* on a scheduled train in 1955. Diesels had replaced the Kings by 1963, but three have been preserved.

WHERE TO SEE IT First of the King class, No 6000 *King George V*, is at the GWR Museum, Swindon, Wiltshire. The two other surviving Kings (No 6024 *King Edward I* and No 6023 *King Edward II*) are at the Didcot Railway Centre in Oxfordshire, where the latter is under restoration. Tel: 01235 817200

▲ *King class loco No 6024 King Edward I.*

TECHNICAL DETAILS
Like their predecessor Castles, Kings were built with four cylinders, two outside and two between the frames, connected to the second and front driving wheels respectively. The Walschaert valve gear of the inside cylinders drives the valves of the outers via levers. Driving wheel are 1.98 m (78 in) in diameter, steam pressure is 17.6 kg/sq cm (250 psi) and total weight 138 tonnes.

BEYER PEACOCK 2-4-0T – ISLE OF MAN

▶ *Beyer Peacock 2-4-0T on the Isle of Man Steam Railway, 1995.*

TECHNICAL DETAILS
The Beyer Peacock 2-4-0 tank locomotive was designed in 1873, and the IoM Railway has four in service. This 2-4-0 has two cylinders and driving wheels 1.14 m (45 in) in diameter. Working steam pressure is 8.54 kg/sq cm (150 psi). Weight is 22 tonnes.

The Isle of Man Steam Railway has four Beyer Peacock 2-4-0 tank locomotives of 1873 design in service. These little engines weigh just 22 tonnes each, three tonnes less than the Dubs and Co 0-6-0T *Caledonia* that has joined them after a rebuild in 1995. The Isle of Man's east coast has one of the world's greatest vintage rail concentrations. The 914 mm (36 in) gauge Isle of Man Steam Railway connects Douglas with Port Erin, and has retained its 19th century-design locos and rolling stock. The Groudle Glen Railway is a 610 mm (24 in) gauge line that climbs 1.2 km through idyllic woods to a windswept clifftop

at Sealion Rocks. Douglas and Ramsey are linked by the Manx Electric Railway, which uses tramcars over 100 years old, and the Snaefell Mountain Railway climbs from Laxey, home of one of the world's biggest waterwheels, to the island's highest point on the island at 620 m (2,036 ft). Finally, the seafront at Douglas has horse-drawn trams!

WHERE TO SEE IT 2-4-0 tanks work the IoM Steam Railway between Douglas and Port Erin, contact IoM Railways on 01624 663366. Any travel agent can supply ferry or flight details for reaching the Isle of Man from mainland UK.

DOUBLE FAIRLIE 0-4-4-0T – WALES

▶ *Merddin Emrys (named after King Arthur's court magician, Merlin), with a train for Porthmadog at Tan-y-Bwlch.*

The Ffestiniog Railway of North Wales bought the first of Robert Fairlie's narrow-gauge power bogie loco-motives in 1869 to handle its heavy slate traffic, and still operates three on today's even heavier tourist trains. *Merddin Emrys* dates from 1879, but *Earl of Merioneth* was built in 1979, and *David Lloyd George* in 1992 – who said steam was obsolete? All three were built at the Ffestiniog's Boston Lodge workshops, which maintain the line's extensive fleet of

locos and rolling stock. The double Fairlie type – essentially two 0-4-0 tank engines set back-to-back, sharing one crew – was used in several countries, but Mallet and Garratt articulated engines proved more efficient, and today the Ffestiniog's Fairlies are unique.

WHERE TO SEE IT The Ffestiniog Railway runs from Porthmadog on the coast to Blaenau Ffestiniog, through rugged scenery. Open daily from Easter to November. Tel: 01766 512340

TECHNICAL DETAILS

Merddin Emrys has two joined boilers above two four-wheel powered bogies, making it an 0-4-4-0T. Because of fire risk in the Welsh forests, the fuel is oil. The loco has four cylinders and boiler pressure is 11.2 kg/sq cm (160 psi). Driving wheels are 84.45 cm (33.25 in) in diameter. The Ffestiniog's gauge is just 600 mm (23.5 in).

SOUTHERN RAILWAY PACIFICS

▲ *Battle of Britain class 257 Squadron with classic air-smoothed or 'spam can' casing.*

TECHNICAL DETAILS

The WC and BB Class engines were built at Southern Railway's works in Brighton and Eastleigh. The driving wheels are 1.88 m (74 in) in diameter. They have three cylinders and run at a steam pressure of 19.7 kg/sq cm (281 psi). Weight is 138 tonnes and length 20.54 m (67 ft 5 in)

The Merchant Navy class, designed by Oliver Bulleid, first appeared in 1941. Disc-type wheels and a squared-off aerodynamic casing gave these 30 engines a unique appearance, and their unconventional features included chain-driven valve gear. The chains tended to stretch, and oil consumption was enormous, but the engines were fast and powerful, and 109 of a smaller but equally effective version were built from 1945 to 1951. The first 48 locos received names associated with the West Country, the remainder with the Battle of Britain. Many of the Pacifics were rebuilt minus the streamlined casings (and fitted with conventional valve gear) in the late 1950s, but eight of the 20 preserved West Country and Battle of Britain locos are in original air-smoothed configuration. All 11 remaining Merchant Navy locos are rebuilt non-streamliners.

WHERE TO SEE IT These handsome SR Pacifics can be seen on many railways across the UK, notably the Bluebell, Great Central, Keighley and Worth Valley, Swanage and Mid-Hants lines. Some engines occasionally work main line excursions, subject to certification.

GREAT RAIL JOURNEYS

◀ *Eurostar loco at the buffers of Gare du Nord, Paris.*

EUROSTAR

A 'must-do' trip for European rail enthusiasts

The story of the Channel Tunnel has been full of financial and political troubles, but by mid-1995, things seemed to be working well, as we found out on a return trip between Waterloo station, London and Gare du Nord, Paris.

Eurostar has a dedicated check-in terminal inside Waterloo, complete with shops and cafes. You pass your ticket through an automatic turnstile, and if you get there with just the 20 minutes or so to spare that's needed, it's straight through x-ray baggage checks into the boarding lines. There are three of them, dividing train entry into sections, which speeds things up. A warning to photographers – there is almost no opportunity to take shots of the locos at Waterloo; better to wait for Gare du Nord, where the trains line up at ordinary platforms.

Inside, the coach decor is dove grey and sunshine yellow; places are allocated so there's no hassle with 'I own your seat' fellow-travellers. Seats are arranged in pairs, either side of the aisle. Compared with an airliner, there's heaps of room,

especially for the legs, but the backs don't recline, more's the pity. The airliner comparison extends to overhead luggage racks and movable reading lamps. Facilities include a train manager (Estelle and her two-person team on our train) French-style standup bar, telephone, baby-changing area and snacks trolley.

ADVANCED RIDE

Eurostars move off with barely a whisper, and start so smoothly that you won't know it unless you look outside the windows. And whisper-quiet running is the overall impression of the journey – a ride that's so far in advance of competing forms of transport it's almost eerie. Moving through leafy Kent, you can hear the clacking of the track, but it's not as slow as press reports had led us to expect and just 98 minutes from Waterloo we pass through the Tunnel entrance. There's no sensation of pressure buildup as we descend (unlike the le Shuttle trains, where you do get some feeling in your ears on the English side). On this occasion, despite Eurostar's promise of a 20-minute crossing, the train glides to a halt

roughly midway 'sous La Manche', with Estelle apologising over the public address system. 'Technical problems not related to our safety', she confirms, then the train moves off, and 32 minutes after entering the Tunnel we pop out into northern France.

HIGH SPEED CRUISING

Within five minutes, the train is accelerating and soon settles down to a cruise speed of 300 km/h, but it's easy to discount the pace, as northern France is very open and there are few nearby objects from which to gauge speed. The quiet ride makes it feel like little more than 200 km/h or so, but a glance at a watch reveals that to reach Gare du Nord on time, we must be running at or around the claimed 300 km/h – 186 mph. And so it proved, for our arrival was just a few minutes late – the time we spent stopped under the Channel. The return run was in first-class – well worth paying extra for, in terms of service, good food, comfort (just two-plus-one seating across the coach) and into Waterloo on time as well. In fact, the unofficial record for the three-hour run was just 2 hrs 41 mins at the time of writing – when traffic on the line is thin, drivers can give the locos their head...

Overall, the Eurostar run has to be a big salute to the French, who pushed ahead with their TGV system, and thus formed the core of what is now a fast-growing pan-European high-speed network.

NIGHTSTAR

By mid-1996, UK passengers should be able to recapture some of the past glories of 'boat trains' to Europe, with the start of a Nightstar service, using the Channel Tunnel. Passengers will be able to board a Waterloo train in the evening, to arrive at, say, Frankfurt at 0710 the following morning. Full sleepers, reclining-seat cars and lounge cars are planned, with the service aiming to set new standards in comfort, service and design. By this time, Waterloo station should be joined by others in the UK, such as Ashford, Glasgow, Plymouth and Swansea.

HEAT AND DUST
Coast-to-coast across Australia

This journey, linking Perth in Western Australia to Sydney in the east, takes you through 3,960 km of contrasting terrain, ranging from city suburbs and mining communities to sun-parched plains and spectacular mountains.

The Indian-Pacific is the diesel-hauled train that runs out of Perth Station, and it was designed from the outset as a cruise liner on rails. For three nights you sleep in single or double compartments ('roomettes' and 'twinettes') to which you can return at any time for a bit of privacy. Otherwise you have a choice of lounge, restaurant, club and bar cars in which to pass the time. The Indian-Pacific dates from 1970, the year after the standard-gauge trans-Australia line was completed. Before then, any rail journey across the continent had to cope with several gauge changes – lines had been built privately, mostly by mining companies, at whatever width track seemed right at the time.

THE LONGEST STRAIGHT
Highlight of the journey, and for some the main reason to do it at all, is the crossing of the vast Nullarbor ('no trees') Plain. It's here that the train runs along the longest stretch of straight track in the world – an amazing 462 km without a bend – while on either side there's searing sun, blue sky, straight-line horizon and parched earth. The sheer immensity is stunning, and as the train pulls to a stop at a line-side halt, you can get off, squint into the sun and feel the dry heat (more than 45°C on a summer's day) sucking the moisture from your body. It's worth it just

▲ EL-class diesel of Australian National Railways. ANR is responsible for the Kalgoorlie-Broken Hill section of the run.

to tell the tale, but it's even better to dive back into the air-conditioned comfort of the Indian-Pacific afterwards!

THE BLUE MOUNTAINS
The last third of the journey takes in scrub-studded mountains such as the Gawler and Flinders Ranges and, nearer Sydney, the Blue Mountains. The 'Blueys' offer some spectacular views and tight bends. When the line was built in the 1860s, the track required a series of switchbacks, the engines pushing and pulling up and down the steeper stretches. Today you can go on a section of this, the steam-hauled Zig Zag railway.

From the Blue Mountains to the coast is an easy run, through the wooded hills and grassy meadows of New South Wales (except in summer, they are green and lush) and then into the sprawl of Sydney itself, before the train eases to a final halt, some 68 hours after leaving Perth.

RAILS IN THE CLOUDS
Peru's mountain railway

The Central Railway of Peru is not only the world's highest line, with a summit reaching 4,783m, but is also one with much spectacular engineering. The 208km route, from Lima to Huancayo, includes zig-zags, double zig-zags, some 67 tunnels and nearly 60 bridges.

BUILDING THE LINE
Although the line was built for carrying metals from the mines in the area, it could easily be named 'the bird-dropping line', for the money to build it came not from rare metals, but from selling guano in Europe as fertilizer. American railroad builder Henry Meiggs was the man responsible for the Central Railway. He signed the construction contract in 1869, claiming that 'anywhere llamas can go, I can take a train'. His engineering work did tame the Andes, but more than 7,000 workers died during the construction, through disease or accidents .

Today, you board the train at Lima's Spanish-colonial style Desamparados Station. Trains are diesel-hauled, though at least one of the British-made 2-8-0 steam locos that used to work the line is still in working order. After leaving central Lima, the train trundles through a wasteland of poverty – shacks and shanty towns stretch into the distance on either side. Eventually however, they are left behind and the diesel's note deepens as the train heads for the mountains. It's all uphill now, until the summit is reached in 172 km or so. As the train climbs, so the views become grander and the line more perilous. Many bridges and viaducts have no parapets, so for passengers the effect can be dizzying – it's often impossible to see any ground under the train unless you actually hang out of a window.

TOWARDS THE TOP
As the train passes the 3,500m mark at Rio Blanco, 120km from Lima, some passengers may feel the effects of oxygen starvation – breathlessness and feeling faint – and it's here that the Central Railway has another unique claim, for there is usually oxygen equipment on board for anyone taken ill. The high point of the line is actually reached inside the 1,177m-long Galera Tunnel, so you can't admire the view until the train emerges into daylight at Galera itself. Here you can photograph the station nameboard, which shows its height, 4,780m, and from here on, it's downhill all the way to Huancayo.

◀ Diesels haul on the Central today.

AFRICA AND THE MIDDLE EAST

The first African railway was the standard-gauge line of 1856 linking Alexandria, Cairo and Suez. Egypt went on to build railways in the Nile Delta and along the river itself. This set the pattern for Africa – lines built by colonial administrations to link European-settled areas and industries, few far inland, and with little thought of joining up with railways of other countries. Diamond tycoon Cecil Rhodes wanted to create a line from the Cape of Good Hope to Cairo in the 1870s. He got less than half way with his dream, and politics and economics has prevented its completion ever since. Today South Africa, Zimbabwe, Tanzania and Kenya have the largest systems. Some countries, notably Gabon, are building new lines, but Africa's size, low population density, difficult terrain and ever-present threat of war do not make the outlook for rail promising. The Middle East, torn by political disputes, has few railways south of Turkey and little through-running between countries. Even so, areas such as Syria and Jordan, are interesting destinations for rail (and especially steam) enthusiasts.

Picture above: GMAM loco near Lootsberg Summit, South Africa.

CLASS 59 — KENYA

The largest type of locomotive ever to work on metre-gauge, Class 59 of East African Railways was built to haul freight and passenger trains uphill for 565 km (350 miles) from Mombasa on the Indian Ocean coast, inland to the capital, Nairobi. The steepest gradient was 1.5 per cent, and given this, plus the tight curves of the line, an articulated Garratt was the only possible choice. Deliveries of 34 locomotives began in 1955 – and all the locos were named after African mountains. They were oil burners, though the basic design could be modified to use coal, if necessary. The layout invented by HW Garratt in 1907, in which a large, efficient boiler is slung between two engine units, not only gave these engines great power and range – 59s could run hard for 14 or 15 hours – but allowed fast running on bends, too. By 1980 all the 'Mountains' were out of service, but one has been preserved for static display.

WHERE TO SEE IT The remaining East African Railways Class 59 Garratt can be seen at the Railway Museum in Nairobi, Kenya.

▲ *EAR Garratt* Mt Gelai, *named after a mountain south of Nairobi.*

TECHNICAL DETAILS

The 4-8-2+2-8-4 Beyer Garratt Class 59, built by Beyer Peacock of Manchester, was more than twice as powerful as any British passenger locomotive. Four cylinders, steam pressure 15.8 kg/sq cm (225 psi). Driving wheels 1.372 m (54 in) diameter. Length 31.737 m (104 ft 2 in) long. Weight 256 tonnes.

CLASS E1300 — MOROCCO

▶ *These GEC Alsthom E1300s were made in conjunction with Moroccan company SCIF, which carried out various jobs, including component assembly, welding, machining and testing. The E1300 can haul an 800-tonne train up 15 per cent grades.*

TECHNICAL DETAILS

Class E-1300 BB, built by GEC Alsthom, France. Based on the 7200 and 22200 classes for the SNCF (French Railways), this 84-tonne loco takes current from an overhead 3kV dc supply to power one traction motor in each bogie, final drive being through shafts. Continuous power rating is 4,000 kW (5,360 hp), and maximum service speed is 160 km/h (100 mph). Sophisticated thyristor control circuitry is installed.

Wearing the handsome body first seen on the SNCF's CC-6500 class of 1970 and later applied to several other Alsthom-built classes, these 18 locomotives were delivered to Moroccan Railways from 1991 for freight and express passenger duties, joining Hitachi-built locos of the E-1100 class. Morocco has a modern system totalling over 1,700 km (1,100 miles) with recent additions, and about half is electrified, using power from hydro-electric schemes in the Atlas mountains. The main line from Rabat to Casablanca is worked by fast Belgian three-car multiple units, and electric locomotives handle air-conditioned 160 km/h (100 mph) expresses on other trunk lines. The main freight cargo in Morocco is phosphates for fertilisers, although coal is mined in the Bouarfa region. The 'Marrakesh Express' fabled in song may not be steam-hauled, but it is part of a system which has much to interest the modern traction fan.

WHERE TO SEE IT On electrified lines between Tangier, Fez and Marrakesh. Morocco is a popular holiday destination, just across the Straits of Gibraltar from Spain.

BLUE TRAIN – SOUTH AFRICA

▲ *Blue Train (here hauled by a trio of Class 6E1 locos) halts at Wellington station, not far from Cape Town.*

One of the world's most luxurious trains, though far from the fastest, the Blue Train of South African Railways covers the 1,608 km (999 miles) between Cape Town and Pretoria in 27 hours. The service dates from 1923, when it ran as the Union Express northbound and the Union Limited southbound. Blue-painted coaches introduced in 1940 gave the train its present name, and the latest rolling stock dates from 1972. The air-conditioned, soundproofed 16-coach train, with an observation car and private sleeper compartments (some have bathrooms), carries 108 passengers in five-star comfort, all on a mountainous, twisting route of 1.07 m (42 in) gauge track. The line is now electrified, except for diesel haulage between Kimberley and De Aar. Steam fans don't miss out entirely though, for the train is shunted between Pretoria station and the maintenance depot by a steam loco! Once a bargain, the twice-weekly Blue Train is now an expensive luxury; even so, it can be booked up for several weeks ahead.

WHERE TO SEE IT The Blue Train runs between Cape Town , Johannesburg and Pretoria, via Beaufort and Kimberley. South African Airways organises Blue Train tours. Tel: 01342 322525.

TECHNICAL DETAILS

Owing to the change of electrification system between Beaufort and De Aar, three classes of electric locomotive are used. They are Class 6E1 Bo-Bo, on 3,000 volts dc, Class 7E Co-Co on 25,000 volts ac and Class 12E Bo-Bo on 3,000 volts dc. The steam shunter is blue-painted Class 19D 4-8-2 No 2749, built by Robert Stephenson and Hawthorn in 1947.

CLASS 25 4-8-4 CONDENSER – SOUTH AFRICA

▶ *Class 25 No 3511 at Houtkraal.*

TECHNICAL DETAILS

Class 25 4-8-4, 1953. A large locomotive for 1.07 m (42 in) gauge, the 25 was built by the North British Locomotive Co in Glasgow, except for a 1948 Henschel-built prototype. Two cylinders power 1.524 m (60 in) driving wheels at a steam pressure of 15.8 kg/sq cm (225 psi). Total weight 238 tonnes. Length 32.77 m (107 ft 6 in). Several non-condensing 25NC locos remain.

South African Railways had a problem on the main line from Cape Town to Johannesburg – trains had to cross the hot, waterless waste called the Karoo, and steam locomotives are notoriously thirsty. The solution lay in the 90 engines of Class 25, which piped their exhaust into a huge, radiator-equipped tender, where 90 per cent of the water was reclaimed by cooling. As steam no longer went up the chimney, a turbine-driven fan was installed in the smokebox to suck air through the boiler tubes, effectively turbocharging the fire. The result was the 'puffers which never puffed' – instead, they whined and roared. Hauling the Blue Train and heavy freights at speed over the long, straight and level Kimberley to De Aar section, the condensers and other steam giants were an impressive sight. Main line scheduled steam in South Africa is no more, but a Class 25 is one of many locos preserved in working order and hauling enthusiast specials.

WHERE TO SEE IT On rail tours administered by the Transnet Museum, Johannesburg, South Africa. Tel: 002 71177 39118.

GMA/GMAM 4-8-2+2-8-4 – SOUTH AFRICA

► *Pouring smoke and steam, a GMAM pulls hard on the Klipsteen-Marmerkop line.*

Among the last South African Railways Garratt-type locos were the 136 engines of the GMA and GMAM classes, almost identical apart from the capacities of their coal bunkers and water tanks. These engines, introduced in 1954 and soon nicknamed 'Gammats', worked on some of the hilliest lines, notably the Cape Town-Port Elizabeth route through the Outeniqua Mountains and over the 1,745 m (5,727 ft) summit of the Lootsberg Pass. One of the GMAMs' first commissions, however, was the Cape Eastern main line, on which they regularly hauled 900-tonne freight trains up the 142 km (88 miles) climb from East

London to Gaika, at gradients of up to two per cent. To prevent damage to tunnel roofs, Gammats had sliding panels which could cover the chimney and deflect the fierce exhaust blast down the sides of the engine. As this tended to suffocate crews, it was little used!

WHERE TO SEE IT The Transnet Museum's fleet at Beaconsfield, Kimberley, includes GMAs and GMAMs available for enthusiast trains. Recently GMAMs worked timber trains on the George-Knysna line, and this may be repeated. A GMAM has been working at the Randfontein Estates Gold Mine.

TECHNICAL DETAILS

GMAM 4-8-2+2-8-4, 35 built by Beyer Peacock 1955-58. Others by Henschel and Sohn, Germany. The GMAM has four cylinders, driving coupled wheels of 1.37 m (54 in) diameter. They work at a steam pressure of 14 kg/sq cm (200 psi). Total weight 195 tonnes. Bunker carries 14 tonnes of coal, tank holds 9,600 litres (2,110 galls) of water. GMAs, carrying less fuel and water, weigh about four tonnes less. Overall length 28.6 m (93 ft 10 in). A water tender, holding 30,917 litres (6,810 galls), can be attached.

HARTMANN 2-8-2 – SYRIA

► *Syrian Railways Hartmann stains the sky with a pall of oil smoke.*

TECHNICAL DETAILS

Hartmann 2-8-2 oil burner. Cylinders are 480 x 500 mm (almost 'square') and steam pressure 12.34 kg/sq cm (176 psi). Driving wheels are 1.07 m (39 in) diameter. Total weight 49 tonnes.

The venerable locomotive shown here – Syrian Railways No 263 – is a relic of World War I, when trains on the Hedjaz Railway ran the gauntlet of raids led by Lawrence of Arabia. Number 263 is an oil-burning 1.05 m (41.38 in) gauge 2-8-2 Mikado, assembled from Hartmann components by the British army, in November 1918. The line it runs on was built in 1908 to carry pilgrims from Damascus to Mecca; it actually stopped 370 km (230 miles) short of Mecca, at Medina in the Hedjaz region. Lawrence's depredations were never made good, and today the line terminates at Maan in Jordan, 467 km (290 miles) south of Damascus. Steam locos still handle much of the

traffic, and considering their tourist potential, they should run for some time to come. Another line, from Damascus to Zebdani and Serghaya, is worked by tank engines, including Swiss-built 0-6-2s of 1896 vintage. The Jordanian part of the Hedjaz has steam locos of British, German, Belgian and Japanese origin.

WHERE TO SEE IT The Syrian part of the Hedjaz Railway ends on the border at Deraa. Jordan operates the line south to Maan. Specials from Damascus also reach Serghaya on the Lebanese border. For tour details, contact 01509 262745. Five Hartmann 2-8-2s survive in Syria; others still work in Java, as Indonesian State Railways class D51.

MODELS AND MEMORABILIA

A better choice than ever before awaits the keen collector

For the keen enthusiast, there has never been a wider choice of collectable material to choose from. Prices have gone up for desirable items, so it pays to think carefully about a purchase. Things are easier for the railway modeller, not only because there is a constant supply of new models coming on the market, but also because buying for future values is rarely at the top of the list for the model train buff.

The latest trains offer plenty of scope for modellers at all gauges. One of the most interesting is the big garden railway 2-6-6-2 Mallet from German maker LGB. Apart from good scale representation (it's based on mineral-hauling loco No 51 from the Uintah Railway Co in the US) it comes with a digital sound board that includes bells, whistles, air pump and even the clang of the fireman's shovel hitting the coal as he loads! Just as much fun is the flickering firelight in the grate, lights and smoke. Garden railways are booming at the moment, and it's easy to understand why when you see models like this. The Uintah is at the top end of this market; beginners can get a ready-to-run starter set for around the £250 mark, a quarter the Mallet's price.

INTERESTING ITEMS FOR COLLECTORS

On the collector's front, the Vintage Toy and Train Museum in Sidmouth, Devon, has all sorts of rare and exotic items on offer. The Museum has made a thing of streamliners through 1995, and among the most interesting is the tinplate Bugatti Autorail train, made in 0 gauge by French Hornby. The real train was quite a flyer, offering 200 km/h (124 mph) speeds in the 1930s, its most striking feature being the raised driver 'pod' sticking up out of the cabin roof. For a real treat (and one that is not too pricey at under £100) try 0-gauge tinplate from ETS in the Czech Republic. 'Elektricks Zeleznice', it says on the wood box of this company's starter set, and when you open the lid, you find a hefty pantograph-equipped electric loco, two wagons and a guard's van. If you like

the unique charm of tin plate models and a big scale this company's offerings are a must-inspect treat.

WRENN OR HORNBY DUBLO?

00-gauge is still the most popular for UK table-top modellers, and collecting rare (and not so rare) productions has become well established. Wrenn models have taken off recently (compared that is, to their Hornby Dublo equivalent) and a 2-6-4T can fetch £200 and more, against just £70-80 for the HD version. As ever of course, buying for investment can be a really tricky strategy – the only real rule to follow is 'buy because you like it'. That way, whatever happens to values, you still have a favourite item. On the limited-edition front, Hornby's *Flying Scotsman*, complete with secondary tender, makes an attractive buy and at the high end of the market, a brilliant newcomer is the Finescale Locomotive Company, whose huge (667 mm long and 3.3 kg weight) gauge 1 BR Pacific *Duke of Gloucester* must rank as one of the finest replicas available. Each one is hand-built and finished with detail extending to wooden planking on the cab floor. Just 100 are planned for production, and it can hardly fail to become a collector's item. FLC can be contacted on 01672 511675.

For railway modellers who like making their own replicas, there are some superb kits available. Among the best is the gauge 1 Peckett 0-6-0 saddle tank from Wychbury Loco Works, a model made largely from heavy etched brass, with white metal fittings, scale wire, tubes and buffer beams all included. For the skilled craftsman, a kit like this is not only a pleasure to make, but also could be an investment for the future. A well-made example (and that's the important thing) will certainly not lose money, and will hopefully repay the time and effort spent in the assembly and paintwork with an enhanced value in years to come. White metal kits need not be hyper-expensive either. A good starter at under £50 is the DJH diesel shunter from Grandspot in County Durham. Everything is

▶ *This Channel Tunnel collection includes tickets, menus and more, plunder from just one London-Paris return journey! The Hornby Eurostar is an HO import from France. The first 2,500 packs have a numbered certificate. Other items include commemorative stamps and timetable.*

▼ *The superb limited-edition FLC Duke of Gloucester, in gauge 1 scale. Craftsmen who assemble the locos sign their names on the insides of panels for posterity.*

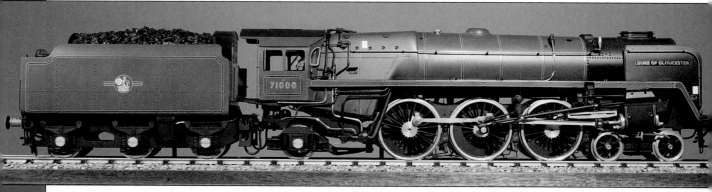

included apart from glue and paint, enabling a first class job to be undertaken by someone starting out. Packaging is good for this type of kit, too – all the components (including gears, wheels, motor and a host of smaller items) are presented in a vacuum-moulded plastic presentation box.

STEAM – IT'S THE REAL THING

Live steam offers plenty to choose from, and this choice of motive power is a natural for garden rail lovers – indeed it's unlikely you'll run steam anywhere else. For the enthusiast, there is nothing to equal a 'real' locomotive running under 'real' power, and with the availability of ready-built locos, live steam is opening up to railway modellers who aren't necessarily model engineers. The sheer size of locos to garden-scale limits the choice somewhat – no Big Boys are offered! Small tanks are very popular, as are US-style logging engines. Butane gas is the main power source for modern live steam locos – the same that's used in a host of DIY tools. To fuel up a steam locomotive, you simply plug in the butane canister's nozzle to the on-board tank, press firmly for a few seconds then the loco is ready to go

COLLECTING STRATEGIES

For collectors of general memorabilia, the choice is wide, but the current cost of many of the 'traditional' collectors' items can create problems. For example, early cast nameplates, though gorgeous and desirable as ever, are now largely beyond the reach of all but the very well-heeled. For the collector starting

out, traditional collectables like these are probably a non-starter initially, on cost grounds alone. A better strategy for the beginner could be to specialise in an area that is not already priced at orbital levels. The Eurotunnel and its trains could make an interesting subject for a collection – on the scale front, there are some excellent models of the rolling stock now available, from well known firms such as Lima, Hornby, Jouef and Kato, with more items in the pipeline. For associated memorabilia, a trip on one of the trains would make a good starting point. Various souvenirs are available to purchase from both the Eurostar and le Shuttle system's shops. On the trains themselves, timetables, tickets and the like are freely available to the enthusiast and will look excellent together as part of a specialised collection – and they are bound to have a collector's value in the future.

▼ *DJM diesel shunter parts on view. This is a good starting point for those new to the art of white metal kit modelling.*

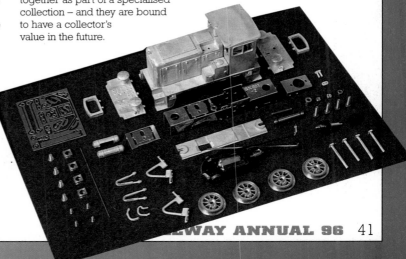

ASIA AND AUSTRALASIA

In the past, railways in Asia and Australasia have mostly concentrated on moving large numbers of people and tonnages of freight rather than on speed. Steam locos are still used on industrial lines in Indonesia, and a few remain in India and Pakistan. China is rapidly modernising its system, though some steam locos are still built for industry. Japan is busy upgrading many lines and building more high-speed railways, while hosting a flourishing preservation movement. New Zealand has a good railway system, and the rail preservation movement is as strong there as in Britain. Australia has a thriving locomotive and rolling stock industry based on the east coast and there is much new construction and modernisation of lines. One of the most startling transformations must be that of the 'Ghan' line to Alice Springs – once it was a ramshackle old track with ancient rolling stock. Now it is a standard-gauge showpiece equipped with state-of-the-art vehicles.

Picture above shows the Darjeeling line, Himalayan peaks beyond.

SPS 4-4-0 – PAKISTAN

▶ *SPS No 3191 pauses at Hariah with a Lalamusa to Shorkot train in January 1993, a scene that has changed little in 70 years or more.*

TECHNICAL DETAILS

SPS class wheel arrangement 4-4-0, gauge 1.676 m (66 in.) Two cylinders with driving wheels 1.88 m (74 in) diameter. Steam pressure is 12.7 kg/sq cm (180 psi). The 0-6-0 SGS class has the same boiler, cylinders and motion, but with smaller driving wheels, 1.562 m (61.5 in) diameter.

Pakistan Railways operates the only 4-4-0 steam locos in everyday service anywhere in the world. Built from 1911 by Armstrong Whitworth, Beyer Peacock and the North British Locomotive Works, these elegant little engines were designed by the British Engineering Standards Association (BESA) as the standard passenger class for the broad-gauge lines of India. The Pakistani survivors are the super-heated version, which was supplied to the Eastern Railway of India and taken over by Pakistan Railways in 1947. Based at Malakwal in central Pakistan, about a dozen engines were still in use in 1995, pulling light passenger trains. A few of a sister class, the goods 0-6-0 SGS, work local freights around Malakwal, including salt and cement trains on the steeply-graded line to Khewra and Dandot.
WHERE TO SEE IT Around Malakwal, Gujrat Province. Contact tour operators for information. In the UK, Liverpool Road Station Museum in Manchester has an SPS on static display.

DARJEELING 0-4-0T – INDIA

Imagine the Ffestiniog Railway of Wales, extended from 22 km (13.7 miles) to 82 km (51 miles), climbing nearly all the way, and you have some idea of the famed Darjeeling Himalayan Railway (DHR) in northern India. The line's steepest gradient is just five per cent but in three places there are tight curves of just 18.3 m (60 ft) radius! The DHR has four loops and the summit at Ghum is at an altitude of 2,148 m (7,407 feet). The line, built to carry tea and passengers, was completed in 1881 and the oldest of its current fleet of 25 0-4-0 tank locos dates from 1888. Each engine carries a crew of five – driver, fireman, coal heaver and two sanders, whose skilled job is to sprinkle sand ahead of the wheels when the rails are slippery, which is much of the time. Despite their age the engines are, of necessity, kept in excellent condition.

WHERE TO SEE IT The DHR runs from Siliguri in Sikkim, India, to the hilltop resort of Darjeeling. It is a rather remote location – some 580 km (360 miles) from Calcutta – but well worth a visit. Contact Steam and Safaris on 01433 620805.

TECHNICAL DETAILS
0-4-0T Class B, Indian State Railways No 799. Built by Sharp Stewart at Queen's Park, Glasgow in 1926 to an 1888 design. Gauge 601 mm (24 in) Two cylinders, driving wheels 660 mm (26 in) in diameter. Steam pressure 10 kg/sq cm (140 psi), water capacity 1,727 litres (380 galls) in the saddle and well tanks. Coal capacity is 1.5 tonnes in a bunker over the boiler. Total weight 15.8 tonnes.

▲ *Crew riding a hard-working DHR locomotive.*

CLASS WP 4-6-2 – INDIA

▶ *A WP of the Central Railway, Indian State Railways, spectacularly decorated for a special working at Kanpur shed.*

TECHNICAL DETAILS

Class WP 4-6-2 Pacific, broad gauge 1.676 m (66 in). Two cylinders, with a steam pressure of 14.7 kg/sq cm (210 psi). Driving wheels 1.705 m (67 in) diameter. Coal capacity 15 tonnes and water capacity 27,000 litres (6,000 galls). Weight 172.5 tonnes. WPs normally carried two firemen.

Despite its somewhat British appearance (the buffers and cab are a giveaway) the first of this 1.676 m (66 in) gauge class actually came from Baldwin of Philadelphia, USA, in 1946. The company built 116, followed by 220 from works in Canada, 30 from Poland and 30 from Austria. The remainder of the 755 locos built were made at Chitteranjan in India from 1963, and the class served with great distinction throughout the Indian broad-gauge network, appearing in the liveries of all India's regions. Despite its extremely purposeful appearance, the bullet nose had more style than function, for speeds on the packed mail and passenger trains pulled by these locomotives rarely rose above 97 km/h (60 mph). Examples of the WP class have been preserved, but none now remain in regular service. Dieselisation and electrification of both broad and metre gauge were expected to be complete by 1995.

WHERE TO SEE IT Many WP locomotives are now laid up and one has been earmarked for future display at Delhi museum. None is available yet for enthusiast working, though it's an odds-on bet that this will happen. For details of various steam tours in India, featuring a variety of locomotives, see the listings section on page 62.

CLASS X 0-8-2T – INDIA

▶ *Large for a rack loco, immaculate X-class No 37388 prepares to push a freight up the long climb to Ootacamund.*

TECHNICAL DETAILS

X-class 0-8-2T by SLM, Winterthur, Switzerland. These unique 48-tonne engines are four-cylinder compounds, in which high-pressure cylinders power the driving wheels. Above the regular mechanism are low-pressure cylinders, which use exhaust steam to drive the rack wheels when required.

Class X locos can be seen on India's metre-gauge Nilgiri Railway, known as the 'Ooty Line', which climbs from Mettuppalaiyam in southern India to the lakeside resort of Ootacamund, 46.3 km (28.75 miles) away and 1,894 m (6,211 ft) higher. The line, opened to Coonoor in 1899 and to Ooty in 1908, is a rack railway in its lower reaches (the grade averages 8.14 per cent) and a conventional line on the 26 km (16 miles) of up to 4.35 per cent above Coonoor. Trains are pushed up the line by Swiss locos built between 1914 and 1925, while signalmen ride on the corners of the leading vehicles to tell the engine crew of hazards on the twisting track ahead. As on all rack railways, a loco precedes its train on the downhill, return journey, to protect it in case of a brake or coupling failure – the loco is always there to stop runaways. Like the Darjeeling, the Ooty railway is likely to remain steam-operated for the foreseeable future.

WHERE TO SEE IT Ootacamund is in the southern state of Tamil Nadu, about 100 km (60 miles) south of Mysore, and can be reached by rail from Madras, Bangalore and Mangalore. The line features strongly in tour company itineraries.

SHINKANSEN SERIES 300 – JAPAN

By the 1950s, the 1.09 m (43 in) gauge railways of Japan's central Tokaido region were becoming hopelessly overloaded. To relieve them, a new standard-gauge high-speed passenger line was built, to take high-tech 'Bullet' trains, far in advance of anything else, anywhere. The line opened in 1964 between Tokyo and Osaka, with trains averaging 160 km/h (100 mph) over the 515 km (320 miles) route. The Shinkansen (meaning 'new network') has now been extended to Kyushu in the south, and will soon run through the Siekan Tunnel to Hokkaido in the north. Japan's railways are now run by regional companies, all working on new lines and stock. Regular speeds are up to 270 km/h (168 mph), but the West Japan company is aiming for a staggering 60 per cent rise to 430 km/h (267 mph) with its

next generation of trains! The Japanese climate can be hard; note that all Shinkansen trains have built-in snowploughs! Old lines are being widened to take new high-speed stock, and a 125 mph train has even been developed for use on improved 1.09 m track.

WHERE TO SEE IT The series 300 trains shown run on the Tokaido Shinkansen line of the East Japan Railway Company, centred on Tokyo. This company also operates Tokoku and Joetsu lines. The Sanyo Shinkansen west of Osaka is run by the West Japan Railway Company.

▲ Shinkansen 300 at speed. Design details include flush windows and doors. The hunt for weight reduction includes seats that weigh less than half previous types.

▼ Three generations of high speed rail in Japan line up for the camera. Series 300 at left, series 100 centre and an original round-nose series 0 'bullet train' on the right.

TECHNICAL DETAILS

The Shinkansen series 300 was introduced in 1992. All Bo-Bo bogies in a 16-car train are motorised, permitting light weight for minimum track wear. Although the original series 0 trains were similarly powered, the series 300 weighs just 396 tonnes, against 876 for the series 0. Power supply is 25 kV ac overhead at 60 Hz. The pantographs are streamlined into roof sections for reduced noise, and normal maximum speed is 270 km/h (168 mph).

CLASS QJ 2-10-2 – CHINA

▶ China's only named locomotive, the QJ-class Marshal Zhu-de, named after Mao Tse-Tung's chief aide. It was photographed at Harbin shed.

TECHNICAL DETAILS

The QJ is based on the 1952 Soviet LV class – much Chinese steam design was a mixture of US, Soviet and Japanese practice. A typical Chinese addition is an air horn to supplement the chime whistle. On the QJ, RM and JS classes, an external steam pipe runs from dome to smokebox in a casing which encloses the chimney. QJ's driving wheel diameter of 1.5 m (59 in) allows a speed of 80 km/h (50 mph) for passenger work.

China, with its huge supplies of coal and vast, cheap workforce, is the world's last major user of steam locomotives. There are no more specialised passenger engines – the last RM Pacifics were retired a few years ago – but large numbers of freight locos, including the magnificent QJ class, remain in service. The Datong locomotive works built an astonishing total of 4,708 of these machines before ceasing in the early 1990s. The class name is 'Qian Jing', meaning 'March Forward', and there is still a good chance of finding these on secondary passenger duties in parts of China. Diesels and electrics are now rapidly displacing steam, however, and soon the QJ will probably be found only on industrial lines. Steam locos are still being built though – for example, the works at Changchun currently builds SY-class 2-8-2s on a limited scale for export and industrial use.

WHERE TO SEE IT QJ locos are scattered through much of China, and Lanzou on the Yellow River has an overhaul establishment. Contact one of the tour companies for details.

SYDNEY MONORAIL – AUSTRALIA

▶ Sydney's AEG-von Roll monorails have seven units per train.

TECHNICAL DETAILS

This system uses a fabricated steel straddle-type monorail. Each bogie in a seven-car train has two pneumatic-tyred riding wheels, four sidethrust wheels and four upthrust wheels bearing on a retaining flange atop the rail. Six bogies are driven from a 500 volts ac three-wire supply, and speed is rated at 33 km/h (21 mph), reducing to 20 km/h on the sharpest bends.

Although Sydney's monorail is just 3.5 km (2.17 miles) long, it is an interesting route. The elevated track, above the streets for about half its length, connects the city centre with the huge leisure and shopping complex of Darling Harbour via the Pyrmont Bridge, and passes several museums and exhibition centres. The line, which opened in 1988, and its six trains, were manufactured by the Swiss firm of von Roll Transport, now part of AEG Transportation Systems. A complete circuit of the six station loop takes about 12 minutes, and two more stations are planned. The operators, TNT, will also build and run Sydney's new Variotram light rail system, and are investigating the possibilities of supplying monorails to various cities in Asia.

WHERE TO SEE IT Sydney monorail loops around a circuit that includes Centrepoint Tower, central Sydney and Darling Harbour. It's a fascinating run, not least because you are above ground level, with a grandstand view! For further information contact TNT Harbourlink. Tel: 0061 2 552 2288.

TANGARA – AUSTRALIA

◄ *A Tangara leaves central Sydney on its way to Wyong.*

TECHNICAL DETAILS

Tangaras operate as four-car multiple units. The two Bo-Bo power cars are in the centre, with much electrical and control equipment in the roof, outboard of the double-deck sections. Power supply is 1,500 volt dc overhead. Max service speed is 130 km/h (80 mph). Pneumatic anti-lock disc brakes supplemented by dynamic and regenerative braking.

Sydney, with its sprawling suburbs, was an early user of double-deck commuter trains, and City Rail has ordered a fleet of stylish new stock, known as the Tangara, to take its service into the 21st century. The cars are air-conditioned – a blessing in the hot 'Oz' summer – and extensively glazed for a good all-round view. Tangaras are hard to beat for a cool and quiet travel experience – outer suburban trains have toilets with facilities for disabled passengers, reversible seats in double-deck sections, and drink-ing fountains. Each four-car train can carry 1,040 passengers for inner suburban or 1,014 for outer suburban services, but the radical styling suggests a much smaller vehicle. The planned initial total of 450 cars, built by Goninan and Co of Newcastle, New South Wales, will include 80 of the outer suburban version.

WHERE TO SEE IT From Sydney Central station, Tangaras run north to Wyong, south to Dapto, and west to Springwood in the Blue Mountains.

CLASS K 4-8-4 – NEW ZEALAND

New Zealand not only has superb railways built over rugged terrain, but also has a long history of locomotive manufacturing. In 1901, Baldwin of Philadelphia built some of the first 4-6-2 locos for New Zealand Government Railways (NZGR), an export across the Pacific Ocean that gave the 'Pacific' wheel arrangement its name. The next upgrade in size was to the bigger 4-8-4 configuration, and the magnificent New Zealand-built Class K was the result. Manufactured from 1932 to 1950 at NZGR's loco shops on both North and South Islands, the 71 engines were of three sub-classes. K and Ka differed only in detail, while six Kbs for the mountain lines of South Island had a booster engine on the trailing truck. Not only could they handle 300-tonne trains on two per cent grades, but on passenger work they achieved 110 km/h (69 mph).

WHERE TO SEE IT Class K locos are preserved at Otahuhu, Seaview and Paekikari on North Island. A Kb is preserved at the Ferrymead Museum, near Christchurch, South Island. Ka No 945 from Paekakariki hauls 17-coach specials at express speeds. Apart from the class Ks, New Zealand has many other fine preserved steam locos.

▲ *Kb No 967 crosses one of South Island's many viaducts.*

TECHNICAL DETAILS

Class K passenger 4-8-4 Northern. Gauge 1.067 m (39 in). Two cylinders and steam pressure 14.1 kg/sq cm (200 psi). Driving wheels 1.372 m (54 in) in diameter. Water capacity 22,700 litres (5,000 galls), coal capacity 8 tonnes , though most Ks (except for the Kbs) were converted to oil burning in the 1940s. Length 21.23 m (69 ft 8 in). Total weight 139 tonnes.

INTO THE FUTURE

The dawn of the new millennium heralds a new age of the train

Two prime areas are providing the catalyst for something of a rail rebirth as the 21st century approaches. Congestion on the roads has finally begun to convince even some anti-rail politicians that there may be transport solutions that don't involve multi-lane highways, and new high-speed rail lines have enabled trains to compete with the airlines on short to medium length routes.

LIGHT RAIL AND TRAMS
Solutions to the problems of urban congestion, especially where commuting is concerned, are a prime concern and light rail and tram systems are leading the way. In much of Europe of course, they have never been ditched, but even in the UK there are signs that at last, a steady renaissance in this type of transport is underway. Manchester and Sheffield have trams again, while other towns such as Croydon, Leeds and Birmingham have them in the planning stages. Rock concerts featuring megastars Bon Jovi and the Rolling Stones in June and July 1995 showed how useful Sheffield's Supertrams could be – thousands of music fans used the trams, and after the 'Stones show, over 5,500 were moved in under an hour. It will be interesting to see whether places

that currently use 'Park and Ride' bus schemes, such as Oxford, will move on to light rail in the future. In fact, Oxford has at least one recent claim to fame in the urban transport stakes – in 1995 planning permission was given for a 20-strong fleet of rickshaws to ply for trade in the city centre! Many cities in mainland Europe are extending their systems or planning new ones. One such is the city of Geneva, in Switzerland. Here, a metre-gauge light rail link is planned, to try to control commuter problems from neighbouring France. At present some 27,000 French workers drive by car across the border to Geneva each morning, then drive home again after work.

FINANCIAL SETBACKS
Airports have been small-scale users of light-rail systems for many years, whether it's the maglev (magnetic levitation) at Gatwick or the shuttle at Paris-Orly. There have been setbacks with high technology though – Birmingham International had to shut down its maglev peoplemover in 1995, as the cost of spares was too high. At present it's a return to buses there until a cheaper replacement has been agreed. In the meantime, the best of the new tram systems not only shift people successfully,

▲ *This design sketch shows the double-deck EMU that will be built for travel around Milan, Italy. Power cars seat 84 with space for the handicapped. Others have seating for 100 and 146.*

▲ *TGV-NG will cruise at around 360 km/h (223 mph) when it enters service in a few years. Testing is planned to start in 1997.*

but are designed to cope with the less fortunate too – SGP of Austria has new trams with ultra-low floors, making them much easier for disabled people to use. It's a lesson that needs applying elsewhere – in the Greater Manchester area, for example, wheelchair passengers can reach only half the stations. Contrast that with New York, where disabled access has been a priority on all public transport for many years – even the buses, on which hydraulic lifts have been a standard fitting for a decade or more.

◀ *Sheffield's Supertram system is a resounding success. Many people are happily leaving their cars behind if going into the city centre at rush hours*

▲ *The new TGV Duplex goes into service in 1996. Using a double-deck design, GEC Alsthom has packed in 45 per cent more people than in a similar size conventional train. Services include nursery, family space, facilities for the handicapped and meeting areas, as well as the usual bar-cafe and telephones.*

Congestion-busting light rail systems are praiseworthy, but it's high-speed lines that grab the headlines. In Europe, TGV and ICE lead the way, while Japan's Shinkansen system has long been a winner. Even in the US, passenger rail is coming back to life again, with much new stock on order, and freight is expanding at the moment, owing to the increase in congestion on the roads.

On the TGV front, new double-deck TGV 2N trains are planned for service entry in September 1996. New power cars replace the present ones and the whole rake of power car and duplex coaches has been given dramatic new external styling by Frenchman Roger Tallon. He is no newcomer to transport design, having been responsible for French trucks as well as recent SNCF rolling stock. Tallon has followed a Eurostar approach where the cab is concerned, having just the single straight-ahead cab windscreen, instead of the wrap-round windows of current TGVs.

NEW-GENERATION TGV

The next step in TGV design will be GEC-Alsthom's TGV-Nouvelle Generation (TGV-NG). This will up maximum speeds to a planned 360 km/h (223 mph)

and will be able to use four different voltages, making it capable of operating virtually anywhere in Europe. The duplex styling will follow on from the TGV 2N, but streamlining will be even more advanced. Careful attention to pantograph aerodynamics and fairings over the wheels will help increase speed, lower power requirements and reduce noise inside the train. TGV-NG is set for testing at the end of 1997.

Double-deck trains are getting very popular as a way of increasing capacity, and Italy's electro-motive units (EMU) for Milan's Passante scheme are planned for service entry in early 1997. The unusual-looking green-and-silver cars are styled by the Italian Pininfarina design consultancy, an outfit better known for its automotive styling for clients that include such famous names as Ferrari and Peugeot.

INTO THE 21ST CENTURY

The next major jump in train speeds is unlikely to come from steel wheels on steel rails – maglev looks like the way things are going. Small scale maglev lines have proved their worth and Germany is planning to build its TransRapid line north from Berlin, with work starting in a few years.

◄► *Steam may be old hat in the real world, but designers still like to dream on. These ideas come from Berlin Art Academy students, who were asked to*

visualise a state-of-the-art steam loco , the lines of which would express the 'power and presence, the essence of steam'. Well, they are certainly a little different!

THE AMERICAS

Between the opening of the first US public railways in the 1830s and the building of lines into northern Canada and the South American Andes, about 80 years elapsed. Rail enjoyed a golden age in the first half of this century, but the explosion of North American car ownership after World War II took rail there into a near-terminal decline. Things are looking up a little now, as road and air congestion has forced a rethink on many routes. Freight too is increasing for similar reasons. For lovers of US rail who cannot make it across the Atlantic, there is a Cornish alternative – at the Dobwalls Miniature Railway near Liskeard, you can ride behind a variety of superb large-scale models of North American locomotives!

Picture shows Union Pacific SD60M diesel leading a freight through the Cajon Pass, California.

BALDWIN 2-8-0 – CUBA

▶ *Steam in Cuba, 1995, as a Baldwin-hauled cane train returns to the mill at Maltiempo.*

TECHNICAL DETAILS

Baldwin 2-8-0. Cuba's steam locos are rebuilt (sometimes radically!) at the mills where they are based. Such 'blacksmith engineering' works well for steam, but is impossible with diesels. No reliable details are available for No 1355 shown here or for most Cuban locos.

The 2-8-0 in the photograph is a 1920 product of the Baldwin company, which built the *Consolidation* in 1866, a name later applied to this wheel arrangement. This rather smaller example, on the 37 km (23 miles), 762 mm (2 ft 6 in) gauge Maltiempo mill line in Cuba, has slide valves in rectangular steam chests, considered old-fashioned even when the loco was built. The island of Cuba has been effectively cut off from the outside world since Fidel Castro's revolution in 1959 and has seen little investment since. Sugar cane is still hauled to many mills by these aging (and in varying states of repair) American-built steam locomotives which are owned by Cuba's Ministry of Sugar, Minaz, and they operate only during the spring harvest. Both standard and

narrow-gauge lines weave through mountain scenery and run alongside roads, though since the breakup of the Soviet Union, which backed communist Cuba against the capitalist USA, it is probably only a matter of time before the island's transport is fully modernised. Tourist facilities are good, and any vintage transport enthusiast (Cuba is full of old 1950s and '60s Yank cars, too) who is able to do so should visit the island while the time-warp lasts.

WHERE TO SEE IT The most interesting steam lines are in the east of the island, but there is also plenty to see nearer the centre. Good resorts are Varadero, Rancho Luna, Playa Larga and Santa Clara. As well as the Baldwin shown here, Cuba also has many Alco locos, plus a few German exports. Contact tour operators for travel information.

ROYAL HUDSON 4-8-4 – CANADA

▶ *Oil-burning Royal Hudson No 2860 is used to haul sightseeing excursions from Vancouver, on the British Columbia Railway.*

TECHNICAL DETAILS

4-8-4 Hudson by Montreal Locomotive Works. Two cylinders drive wheels 1.905 m (75 in) diameter. Steam pressure 19.3 kg/sq cm (275 psi). Coal burners carried 21 tonnes of fuel and 54,600 litres (12,000 galls) of water. Weight 299 tonnes. Length 27.67 m (90 ft 10 in).

Intense competition with Canadian National Railways led the Canadian Pacific to buy 20 4-6-4 Hudson-class H-1 locomotives in 1931. For five months, the 'Royal York' Toronto-Montreal express was the world's fastest scheduled train, before the GWR's 'Cheltenham Flyer' regained the title. The H-1 had an immense range, reducing the number of engine changes needed on long runs across Canada. Thirty of a semi-streamlined version, in 19th century CPR-livery black and tuscan red, appeared in 1937. Ten more were delivered in 1938, and five oil-burners in 1940. After specially-painted No 2850

pulled the Royal Train in 1939 (for a Canadian visit by King George VI and Queen Elizabeth), all the later classes carried royal insignia on valances and tender. Regular steam on the CPR ended in 1960, but an H-1b and four 'Royal Hudsons' have survived.
WHERE TO SEE IT There are H-1s in various places, including the Canadian National Railway Museum, Delson, Quebec and National Museum of Science & Technology, Ottawa. For excursions contact the British Columbia Railway, Vancouver. Tel: 001 604 984 5246 and the Royal Hudson Steam Train, Vancouver. Tel: 001 604 688 7246.

AMERICAN TYPE 4-4-0 – USA

The outside-cylinder 4-4-0 evolved in America during the 1840s and 1850s. With suspension designed for rough track and all moving parts easily accessible, colourful 'eight-wheelers' comprised the majority of North American loco production up to the 1880s. Six- and eight-coupled engines took over as loads increased, and by 1890 4-4-0s were built only for fast passenger work. In 1893, engine No 999 of the New York Central Railroad claimed an unofficial record of 181 km/h (112.5 mph) hauling a special four-car Empire State Express. At the other end of the speed scale, the small Virginia & Truckee Railroad of Nevada (1869-1950) sensibly maintained a sense of tradition, and four of its six 4-4-0s survive. All have appeared in Western films, and one of them, No 11 *Reno*, still does so.

WHERE TO SEE IT The *Inyo* engine shown here and No 18 *Dayton* are both based at the Nevada State Railroad Museum, Carson City, Nevada. Tel: 001 702 6876953. V&T No 12 *Genoa* is at the California State Railroad Museum, Sacramento, and is also steamable. Many other 19th century 4-4-0s are preserved, with varying degrees of authenticity.

▲ *Virginia and Truckee's No 22 Inyo (nicknamed Brass Betsy) at the Nevada State Railroad Museum, Carson City.*

TECHNICAL DETAILS

This engine was made by the Baldwin Locomotive Works, Philadelphia, in 1875. It is a wood-burner with spark-arresting 'bonnet' smokestack and two cylinders. Driving wheels are 1.45 m (57 in) in diameter. Length 15.29 m (50 ft 2 in), weight 51.44 tonnes, steam pressure 9 kg/sq cm (130 psi).

BALDWIN K36 – USA

◄ *Baldwin K36 No 481 heads for the canyons with a train of vintage coaches.*

TECHNICAL DETAILS

Baldwin K36 No 481 was built for the Denver & Rio Grande Western in 1925. A two cylinder coal-burner with 1.118 m (44 in) driving wheels and steam pressure of 13.65 kg/sq cm (195 psi), it is a powerful locomotive. It looks huge on the narrow rails of the Durango & Silverton. The Cumbres & Toltec also uses ex-D & RGW locos.

The scenic Durango & Silverton Railroad was originally an extension of the Denver & Rio Grande Western Railroad's Alamosa-Durango branch. This was built in 1881 to serve silver mines in the valley of the Los Animos river. The railroad has a fleet of three Alco and three Baldwin engines, one of them a unique conversion from a standard gauge K37. The 0.914 m (3 ft) gauge line climbs north from Durango for 72 km (45 miles) into the heart of the Rocky Mountains, often on narrow ledges high above the river. Nowadays the passengers are not miners but sightseers and rail enthusiasts, eager to ride in elegant yellow vintage coaches behind some of the world's most powerful surviving narrow-gauge locos. Another section of the old line to Alamosa is now the 103 km (64 miles) Cumbres & Toltec Scenic Railroad, famous for its winter excursions behind a spectacular plume of snow from a hard-working rotary snowplough!

WHERE TO SEE IT The Durango & Silverton Narrow Gauge Railroad is at Durango, Colorado. Tel: 001 303 247 2733. The Cumbres & Toltec is at Chama, New Mexico. Tel: 001 505 756 2121.

CHALLENGER CLASS 4-6-6-4 – USA

TECHNICAL DETAILS

4-6-6-4 Mallet articulated. Rear drivers and cylinders are fixed, the front set being attached to them by a vertical hinge. Four cylinders at a steam pressure of 19.7 kg/sq cm (280 psi). Driving wheels are 1.75 m (69 in) in diameter. Length 37.16 m (121 ft 11 in). Weight some 486 tonnes, oil burners some 28 tonnes less.

Easily the largest locomotives ever to haul passenger trains, the Union Pacific's 105-strong 'Challenger' class articulated 4-6-6-4s were built by the American Locomotive Company (Alco) in two batches between 1938 and 1944. The 65 engines of the second batch had larger grates, higher steam pressure and a modified pivot for the forward power unit, giving better adhesion. There were both coal- and oil-burning Challengers; some were converted more than once. As well as freight working, they could be rostered for passenger service at speeds of up to 112 km/h (70 mph). Some locos appeared in the Union Pacific's grey passenger livery, but the preserved oil-burning No 3985 is in standard black. This locomotive is maintained in working order by the UP, and works the occasional special train.

WHERE TO SEE IT Together with other historic working UP locos, Challenger No 3985 is stabled at Cheyenne, Wyoming; a major overhaul is scheduled to start in 1996. A static example, No 3977, is at Cody Park, North Platte, Nebraska.

▲ *Union Pacific's Challenger No 3985 is now the world's largest operating steam locomotive.*

FEF 4-8-4 – USA

Elegantly proportioned, with tapered side rods and a minimum of external plumbing, the 'FEF' (Four-Eight-Four) locomotives were the Union Pacific's last purpose-built passenger steam engines. Alco built 20 of them (FEF-1) in 1938, 15 with bigger driving wheels, cylinders and tenders (FEF-2) the following year, and the last ten (FEF-3), with minor modifications, in 1944. As with many late American steam locos, the frame and cylinders were a single steel casting, and, apart from automatic stoking and power reversing gear, the design was kept very simple. FEFs converted to burn oil during post-war coal strikes could hit 177 km/h

▲ *With support tender and double-heading with a diesel loco, UP No 8444 roars through Milford, Utah, on 1 May 1989.*

(110 mph) with heavy expresses. The last of the FEFs were withdrawn in 1958 and just four survive today. The last example, No 8444 (originally 844), is expected to complete a major overhaul shortly, ready for main line enthusiast work in 1996.

WHERE TO SEE IT FEF-1 No 814 is at Dodge Park, Council Bluffs, Nebraska. No 8444 is shedded at the Union Pacific roundhouse in Cheyenne, Wyoming, with No 838 kept as a spares donor.

TECHNICAL DETAILS

Wheel arrangement of the FEF series was the 4-8-4 Northern type. The front drivers had side-play built in, to aid cornering on tight curves. The FEF-2 and 3's two cylinders powered driving wheels 2.32 m (80 in) in diameter. Steam pressure 21 kg/sq cm (300 psi). Fuel capacity for oil-burners was 27,240 litres (6,000 gal), while coal burners carried up to 23 tonnes. Water capacity 90,800 litres (20,000 galls) Total weight for a coal burner 412 tonnes. Length overall 34.7 m (113 ft 10 in).

GE AMD-103 GENESIS – USA

The Genesis class of diesel locomotives was introduced in 1993, to haul inter-city trains of Amtrak, the US national passenger network. Genesis comes in two types, the diesel Genesis I and the new Genesis II, which can also use third-rail supply. The operating company Amtrak was set up by the US government in 1970, to save what was left of passenger services, at that time a fast-disappearing asset. Amtrak took over the passenger stock of participating railroads, and introduced new coaches and locos of its own. It owns some lines but otherwise uses the tracks of the old private companies. Even so, Amtrak covers only 13 per cent of the US rail system, and despite efforts to sell its benefits, was cutting some services in 1995.
WHERE TO SEE IT Genesis locos haul named expresses on most of Amtrak's non-electrified routes, from Chicago to Florida and across to the Pacific coast. Genesis II is designed to operate into New York, where pollution laws allow only electric locomotives, and will also serve Chicago, Montreal and Toronto.

▲ *Amtrak's GE-hauled 'Desert Wind' en route eastbound from Los Angeles to Chicago.*

▼ *At Salt Lake City, the train combines with the California Zephyr from Oakland.*

TECHNICAL DETAILS

General-Electric AMD-103 Genesis I Bo-Bo has a 16-cylinder 2,983 kW (4,000 hp) diesel engine, driving dc traction motors. Weight 123.5 tonnes, fuel capacity 8,327 litres (2,200 US galls). Genesis II can use 650 volts dc third-rail supply. To house the extra equipment, it has a smaller engine and less fuel capacity.

GM F7 'WARBONNET' – USA

TECHNICAL DETAILS

GM Electro-Motive Division F7A and F3B. Each unit has one 16-cylinder diesel engine of 1,120 kW (1,500 hp), driving four electric traction motors. Wheel arrangement Bo-Bo. Length A unit 15.44 m (50 ft 8 in), B unit (booster) 15.24 m (50 ft). A units weigh in at just over 111 tonnes, boosters half a tonne less.

The Atchison, Topeka and Santa Fe Railway (not all US lines are 'Railroads') bought these 160 km/h (100 mph) diesel-electric locos in 1949 for fast passenger service, including the celebrated 'Super Chief' express between Chicago and Los Angeles. Among first-generation American diesels, cabless B types, known as boosters, were marshalled between A units to make up the required power. The production run of the series was long – 2,261 F7As and 694 F3Bs were made. In 1986 the Santa Fe's 14-strong collection of preserved steam and diesel locos was

donated to the California State Railroad Museum and two years later the 'Warbonnet' diesels were meticulously restored. The splendid paintwork is based on a stylised Native American headdress, hence the name. These operating locomotives are now a powerful magnet for diesel fans.

WHERE TO SEE IT At the California State Railroad Museum at Sacramento, California, which has a huge collection, with many working engines. An absolute must for rail fans on holiday in the region. Tel: 001 916 448 4466..

▲ The California State Railroad Museum's ex-Super Chief diesel looks magnificent in the traditional Santa Fe Warbonnet livery.

GS CLASS 4-8-4 – USA

TECHNICAL DETAILS

GS-4, wheel arrangement 4-8-4 Northern type. Two cylinders with an extra two-cylinder booster engine mounted underneath the firebox for extra power on steep and long inclines. Driving wheels 2.3 m (80 in) diameter, and steam pressure 21.1 kg/sq cm (305 psi). Total weight just over 400 tonnes. The GS-4 is an oil-fired design, with a capacity of 22,246 litres (4,900 galls) of oil and about 89,000 litres (19,600 galls) of water. Unusually for a Northern, the leading pair of driving wheels have built-in side-play to aid cornering on tight bends.

▲ GS-4 No 4449 (left) with Southern Pacific No 2472 on display at the Sacramento Rail Fair, 3 May 1991.

Semi-streamlined and painted to match the 568-tonne 'Daylight' expresses they were built to haul, the Southern Pacific Railroad's GS-4 class must have looked and sounded magnificent pounding up the steep grades and round the sharp bends of the 756 km (470 miles) Los Angeles-San Francisco line. Quick-acting, electrically-controlled air brakes were standard, as was a tonne of sand to combat wheel slip. Mounted under the firebox and driving wheels on the rear truck, was a secondary booster engine which could be turned on (using steam from the main boiler) to give extra punch on long or steep gradients. Sixty locos formed classes GS-2 to GS-6.

They were all built by the Lima Locomotive Works, Ohio, between 1937 and 1943, and they spread throughout the SP system and onto the Western Pacific Railroad. GS-6s were painted black all over, but the other classes kept their spectacular livery until withdrawal in the 1950s.

WHERE TO SEE IT GS-4 No 4449 is owned by the City of Portland, Oregon and is maintained in running order by the Southern Pacific at Portland. Tel: 001 503 986 4129. Static exhibit GS-6 No 4460 is in the Museum of Transportation, St Louis, Missouri. Tel: 001 314 965 7998.

MT WASHINGTON COG RAILWAY – USA

TECHNICAL DETAILS

In the Marsh rack system a central pinion, geared to a jackshaft driven by the four cylinders, engages a ladder-like rack between the rails, leaving the running wheels unpowered. During the climb up the peak, engines use a tonne of coal and more than 18,000 litres (1,000 galls) of water, pushing one passenger car.

◀ In 1869, this cog railway was regarded as a marvel of new technology and you'll still be impressed today. The ride to the top and back takes about three hours.

Although rack railways are usually associated with Europe, particularly the Alps, the very first was actually built in the USA. Sylvester Marsh demonstrated his rack system in 1866, and it was used on a 1.4 m (55 in) gauge tourist railway up Mt Washington in northern New Hampshire. The line opened in 1869 and is still in service today. It climbs from 783 m (2,569 ft) to the summit at 1,917 m (6,288 ft) in 5.3 km (3.3 miles). The gradient averages 25 per cent, steepening in places to 37 per cent. Parts of the line are carried on wooden trestlework, and the railway has successfully retained something of its 19th century atmosphere. The vertical-boilered prototype locomotive *Peppersass* of 1866 is on static display at the base station. Mt Washington is not the only US rack railway – there is another in Colorado, the Manitou and Pike's Peak line.

WHERE TO SEE IT Route 302, Mt Washington, New Hampshire, USA. Open May to October. For details call 001 603 846 5404 or toll-free in the US 1-800 922 8825 Ext 6.

SAN FRANCISCO CABLE CAR – USA

The San Francisco cable car system is famous the world over, and is an excellent example of an environment-friendly down-town light railway that many more cities could use. The designer was English-born Andrew Smith Hallidie, who was inspired by the fact that many San Francisco streets were too steep for horse-drawn street cars. His answer to the problem was a series of cars, powered by an under-ground cable that covered the route in a continuous steel loop. This extremely original system is still in use today. A powerhouse keeps the cable running at a smooth and constant 14.5 km/h (9 mph) and a cable car moves along by means of a mechanical clamp, which grips the cable when required. The cars can be turned round using a combination of turntable and human muscle power.

WHERE TO SEE IT The cable cars operate in central San Francisco, California. The Mason-Hyde, Powell-Hyde and California Street lines carry thousands of locals and visitors daily between such famous San Francisco sights as Fisherman's Wharf, Chinatown and Union Square.

◀ On the streets of San Francisco, passengers cling onto the running boards of cable car No 15. Out in the bay, you can see the famed Alcatraz prison, now yet another haunt for SF's tourist visitors.

TECHNICAL DETAILS

Cable cars roll on two four-wheel bogies, with a grip that fits into a narrow slot between the rails. Closing the grip catches the cable that runs in the slot and the car moves forward. The cars have both covered and open seating, with a verandah at the back. Maximum speed is 14.5 km/h (9 mph).

SHAY LOGGER – USA

The locomotive shown here was built by the Lima Locomotive Works for use on steep and twisting logging railways. Based on principles developed by Ephraim Shay in 1877, the engine has all wheels driven by gears, like a modern diesel or electric loco. Three cylinders mounted vertically amidships drive a shaft, which turns the wheels via bevel gears on their faces. The exhaust has to be seen and heard to be believed, but the loco is powerful and sure-footed – necessary requirements for logging work. The engine in the photo above is shown working on the narrow-gauge – 0.914 m (36 in) – Georgetown Loop Railroad in the US Rocky Mountains. The line climbs 195 m (638 ft) in just over 3 km (2 miles) by looping around the bottom of Clear Creek Canyon and crossing over itself on the spectacular Devil's Gate Bridge. Well worth a visit, the line also features conventional steam locomotives.

WHERE TO SEE IT Shay loggers can be seen in many places in the US. The one featured above is at the Georgetown Loop Railroad, Georgetown, Colorado. It is open during the summer season. Tel: 001 303 569 2403/303 670 1686.

▲ *A 1927 Shay toils its smoky way uphill on the Georgetown Loop Railroad in Colorado state.*

TECHNICAL DETAILS
Shay locomotives have two or three four-wheel power bogies, driven by a telescopic jointed shaft running the length of the engine on the right-hand side. To make room for this drive system, the boiler is offset to the left. Three cylinders, steam pressure 14.07 kg/sq cm (200psi), with driving wheels 81.28 cm (32 in) diameter. Oil burner.

RAIL RECORDS

A look at the long history of rail and rail technology

TRACKWAYS AND WOODEN RAILS

The very first 'trackways', built to guide vehicles along a permanent way, are thought to date back as far as the ancient Greece of more than 4,000 years ago. Archaeologists have found evidence of stone guide blocks, with cut grooves in which wheels would have fitted.

In Europe, the railways date back to the 1600s, for mineworking. The tracks were usually of wood. It was not until 1787 that the first steel rails were laid – at a coal mine in Sheffield, England.

THE FIRST STEAM LOCOS

Cornish engineer Richard Trevithick devised the first steam locomotive, for hauling work at the Pen-y-Darren iron-works in South Wales. In a run on 21 February 1804, 70 men climbed aboard a train pulled by Trevithick's loco (actually his second machine – the first was not a success), to become the first steam railway passengers. As a working loco, the machine had a problem – its five-tonne weight was too great for the fairly brittle cast-iron rails used at Pen-y-Darren.

George Stephenson's pioneering work was more successful. His first loco could haul 30 tonnes of coal at walking pace. The 1825 *Locomotion* could hit speeds up to 32 km/h (20 mph). In France, pioneer Marc Seguin used a multiple fire-tube arrangement, which brought water to the boil quickly and evenly.

RAIL TAKES OVER THE PLANET

By the 1820s, railway construction was

◄ *The first German railway opened up for business in 1835. This engraving of the time shows the crowd who assembled for the maiden journey.*

► *Japan's Shinkansen was the first modern system to use dedicated track, enabling sustained high speed running.*

becoming a boom industry. In Europe, Germany's first railway opened in 1835; the same year the Brussels-Malines line opened in Belgium; the first public steam service opened in France between Paris and Le Pecq two years later.

North America saw boom years too, with the famous 'golden spike' being driven to complete the transcontinental link in 1869. It could have happened somewhat earlier actually, but the two companies building the line from opposite directions were paid by the amount of track laid. No agreement had been reached with the US government (which was paying the bills) as to the exact joining spot, so they put down 362 km (225 miles) of side-by-side roadbed before finally stopping.

Other notable railway 'firsts' include the first line to open in Africa, a 208km (129

miles) run between Alexandria and Cairo, in 1856, and the start of Japan's railway system in 1872, with a line that ran between Yokohama and Sinegawa on the island of Honshu.

THE LURE OF SPEED

Before the coming of the railways, the fastest you could travel was on the back of a fast horse – say 65 km/h (40 mph) or so for a short distance. Early trains were lucky if they could manage 50 km/h (30 mph) but in a few decades, speeds were triple this and more. In 1893, the American 4-4-0 Number 999 locomotive hauled a special four-car Empire State Express train at a reported 181 km/h (112.5 mph), becoming the fastest man-made object on Earth in the process. Today, the world speed record for conventional rail traction is held by a French TGV, at 513.3 km/h (320 mph).

TRIAL OF STRENGTH

A big competition was held in October 1829 – at stake, a contract to build locos and rolling stock for the new Liverpool and Manchester railway. The entries included a machine powered by two men, another had one live horse power. Of the steam locos, head-and-shoulders winner was the yellow-painted *Rocket*, entered by George and Robert Stephenson, with their backer Henry Booth. Other entries blew joints and suffered failed pumps, so the reliable *Rocket* rolled away with a fat £500 prize and the railway contract.

◄ *Close-up view of the rivetted firebox of Stephenson's* Rocket.

BUSIER AND BUSIER

The statistics of railway running are quite remarkable, and those of Japan's system, the world's busiest, even more so. The famous Tokaido-route bullet trains opened for business in November 1965, becoming the world's first scheduled train service to offer average running speeds of more than 161 km/h (100 mph), a world-beating achievement at the time. The line boomed, and by the mid-1970s a staggering 1,000 million passengers had travelled the route, over 800,000 of them on one particularly busy day in 1975. Services nearer home could learn a thing or two – bullet services are planned with just a 15 second delay-time built in. So far as mere numbers go, the the honours must go to the East Japan system, which regularly carries around 20 million passengers a day.

BIGGER AND BIGGER

Rail giants – especially steam locos – earn a special place in the hearts of rail fans. Biggest of the lot were the 4-8-8-4 Big Boys of the US Union Pacific. These UP giants weighed in at an awe-inspiring 508 tonnes, and had a freight-pulling capacity of 5,000 tonnes-plus. Ironically, the multi-wheel layout, designed mainly to reduce axle load on the track, didn't do the job as well as intended. The UP Railroad still had to replace much of the track that the Big Boys used regularly.

RAILWAY MUSEUMS

The make time to see if you visit list!

This selection of world rail museums gives you an idea of what's on offer. Non-British telephone numbers, where given, include international codes from the UK.

AUSTRALIA
Various museums are administered enthusiastically by the Australian Railway Historical Society, PO Box 1119, Toowong, Queensland 4066. Tel: 00617 371 4231

BELGIUM
Belgian Railway Museum, Brussels Nord Station, Vooruitgangstraat 76, 1210 Brussels.

CANADA
National Museum of Science and Technology, 1867 St Lawrence Boulevard, Ottawa, ON K1G 5A3.
Tel: 001 613 991-3044
Canadian Railway Museum, 120 St Pierre Street, Saint-Constant, Quebec PQ J5A 2G9. Tel: 001 514 632 2410

DENMARK
Danish Railway Museum, Dannebrogsgade 24, 5000 Odense.
Tel: 004 566120164

EGYPT
Cairo Railway Museum, Ramses II Station.

FRANCE
Musee Francais du Chemin de Fer, 2, rue Alfred de Glehn, 68200 Mulhouse.
Tel: 0033 89 42 25 67

GERMANY
Eisenbahnmuseum Bochum-Dahlhausen, Dr C Otto-Strasse 191, 4630 Bochum 5. Tel: 0049 234 492 516
DB Verkehrsmuseum, Lessingstrasse 6, 8500 Nuremberg 70.
Tel: 0049 911 219 24

GREAT BRITAIN
Birmingham Railway Museum, 670 Warwick Rd, Tyseley, B11 2HL.
Tel: 0121 707 4696
GWR Museum, Faringdon Rd, Swindon SN1 5BJ. Tel: 01793 493 189
Glasgow Museum of Transport, Kelvin Hall, Glasgow, Scotland G3 8DP
National Railway Museum, Leeman Rd, York YO2 4XJ. Tel: 01904 621261
Science Museum, Exhibition Rd, South Kensington, London SW7 2DD.
Tel: 0171 938 8000
Ulster Folk and Transport Museum, Cultra, Holywood BT18 0EU Tel: 01232 428428
Welsh Industrial and Maritime Museum, Pier Head, Bute Street, Cardiff CF1 6AN.
Tel: 01222 481919

GREECE
Athens Railway Museum, 4, Siokon Str, 301 Liosson Street, 10443, Athens.
Tel: 00301 524 6580

HOLLAND
Nederlands Spoorwegmuseum, Maliebaan Station. 3581 XW Utrecht.
Tel: 0031 30 306206

INDIA
Indian Railway Museum, Shantipath, Chanakyapuri, New Delhi 110021.

ITALY
Leonardo da Vinci Museum, Via San Vittore 21, 20123 Milan.

JAPAN
Tokyo Transportation Museum, 25, 1-chome, Kanda-Sudacho, Chiyoda-ku, Tokyo 101. Tel: 0081 3325 8481.

KENYA
Kenya Railways Museum, PO Box 30121, Nairobi.

NEW ZEALAND
Museum of Transport and Technology, PO Box 44114, Great North Road, Western Springs, Auckland 2.
Tel: 0064 9 860 199.
The Engine Shed, Paekakariki, PO Box 46-012, Park Avenue, Lower Hutt.
Tel: 0064 4758 701.

POLAND
Muzeum Kolejnictwa, PO Box 44, ul Towarova 1, 00958 Warsaw.
Tel: 0048 22 2004 80

SOUTH AFRICA
Transnet Museum, PO Box 3753, Johannesburg Station 2000.

SPAIN
Spanish Railway Museum, Paseo de las Delicias 61, 28045 Madrid.
Tel: 0034 1527 3080/3121

SWEDEN
Swedish Railway Museum, PO Box 571, Ralsgatan 1, 80108 Gavle 1.
Tel: 0046 26 10 64 48

SWITZERLAND
Verkehrshaus der Schweiz, Lidostrasse 5, 6006 Lucerne.
Tel: 0041 41 314 444

USA
California State Railroad Museum, 111 I Street, Sacramento, CA 95814.
Tel: 001 916 448 4466
Smithsonian Institution, Constitution Avenue, Washington DC 20560.
Tel: 001 202 357 2700
Illinois Railway Museum, Box 427, Union, IL 60180. Tel: 001 815 923 4000
B&O Railroad Museum, 901 West Pratt St, Baltimore, MD 21211.
Tel: 001 410 752 2490
Nevada State Railroad Museum, Carson City, NV 89710.
Tel: 001 702 697 6953
Steamtown National Historic Site, 150, South Washington Av, Scranton, PA 18503.
Tel: 001 717 340 5202
Virginia Museum of Transportation, 303, Norfolk Ave, Roanoke, VA 24016.
Tel: 001 703 342 5670

ZIMBABWE
Zimbabwe Railways Museum, PO Box 596, Bulawayo.

TECHNICAL TERMS EXPLAINED

We have tried to avoid extensive use of technical terms in this overview of world rail, but the following may require some explanation.

AC Alternating current, constantly switching between positive and negative, allows higher voltages to be used than dc. This allows feeder stations to be further apart and is more efficient.

ARTICULATED These locomotives have some or all of their driving wheels in bogies. Steam 'artics' include the Fairlie, Mallet and Garratt types.

BOGIE To avoid damaging the track on curves, locos, coaches and wagons longer than about 10 metres (less on narrow gauge) have wheels set in swivelling trucks called bogies, one at either end. Bogies support all modern diesel and electric locomotives and the ends of most larger steam engines.

CLASS A group of locomotives built to the same design and specifications., though later rebuilding can make some examples look somewhat different. A class usually has its own number series, and engines are sometimes named according to a single theme.

COUPLING RODS On most steam, and some diesel and electric locos, the driving wheels are coupled together by rods attached to cranks, spreading the power to all driving axles. This is not to be confused with the couplings which connect vehicles in a train.

CRANKS These are levers on the driving axle or wheels of a steam loco which allow the push and pull of the pistons and their connecting rods to turn the wheels. Think of the pistons as the legs of a cyclist, the cranks as pedals! A diesel engine may have one or more crankshafts geared to an electric generator or hydraulic transmission.

CYLINDER In steam and diesel locos, steam or burning oil/air mixture pushes tight-fitting pistons along tubular spaces called cylinders, just as a bullet is pushed along a gun barrel. Rods and cranks take the power to wheels (in the case of steam) or a generator (in a diesel). Diesel engines require many cylinders to provide smooth levels of thrust, but a steam loco needs only two, three or four.

DC Direct current, used in third-rail and early overhead power supply systems. Feeds a steady electric current to electric loco or power car.

FLANGE The raised rim on the inside edge of a railway wheel, which guides the vehicle along the rail.

GAUGE On railway tracks, is the distance between the inside edges of the rails. It is measured with a stick called, logically enough, a gauge. 'Standard gauge' is the commonest, at 56.5 inches between the rails.

OUTPUT In a diesel locomotive, this is the design maximum power of the engine. Some power is lost in the transmission system, on its way to the drive wheels. Electric locos have a continuous power rating (usually the one quoted) and a higher output, one that can be sustained for an hour before the motor overheats. Sophisticated modern electronic control systems feed current to motors in ultra-precise pulses, saving energy yet obtaining more power at the same time.

▲ This cross-section of a 1930s Hiawatha loco shows the path steam takes (coloured arrows) through the boiler (1) and dome (2) down to the cylinders (3), finally exhausted through the chimney (4).

PANTOGRAPH A sprung roof frame carrying the contact bar of an electric loco using an overhead supply.

STEAM PRESSURE Usually quoted as the pressure of steam in the boiler. Passing through the regulator or throttle valve on its way to the cylinders, it is at a varying (but lower) pressure.

TRAIN Any set of passenger or freight vehicles coupled together and propelled by a locomotive or built-in motors. A locomotive by itself is *not* a train, any more than a horse is a cart. Most 'train spotters' are actually locospotters!

TRANSMISSION The method by which power is transferred from motor to wheels. Steam locos use a direct form, from cylinder to connecting rods. Diesel locos usually use the engine to power electric motors, fed by a dynamo or alternator. Some, notably in Germany, use hydraulics – fluid circulated by a pump drives turbines geared to the axles.

VALVE GEAR The machinery in a steam loco that controls the valves letting steam in and out of the cylinders. In both forward and reverse, it can be set to give a shorter valve action – saving steam once running speed is reached. The two commonest types of valve gear are Stephenson's and Walschaert's.

Have you enjoyed this annual?
Why wait a year until the next!

KEEP ON TRACK
with

Published since 1897 *MAGAZINE*

Every month, *Railway Magazine* keeps you bang up to date with the latest news and developments in the exciting and rapidly-changing world of railways.

If this annual has whetted your appetite and made you want to learn more, then *Railway Magazine* is for you!
Whether it's steam, diesel or electric, Britain's biggest-selling all-in-one railway journal has the lot, coupling topicality with the best of history and nostalgia – and packed with super photographs!

MAKE SURE YOU DON'T MISS A SINGLE COPY BY BECOMING A SUBSCRIBER.
Not only do you get every issue delivered to your home, but you also save money – post & packing are free and each issue costs just £1.98 compared with £2.20 in the shops.

Becoming a subscriber is easy. Just fill in the form below or phone our subscription hotline. Subscriptions also make wonderful Christmas or birthday presents!

We look forward to welcoming you on board.

Nick Pigott
Editor *Railway Magazine*

PS *Railway Magazine* will be **100 years old in 1997** and it promises to be a very special year.
Subscribe now and make sure you are a part of our centenary year!

INDEX

TOUR COMPANIES

Special travel operators have opened up in recent years, their aim to provide tours for rail fans. Here are some of them. Telephone numbers are up to date at the time of writing. In case of difficulty contact your local travel agent.

Bales Escorted Tours
Tel: 01306 885991
Offers various rail trips that include the Canadian Pacific and 'Rocky Mountaineer' trips through the Rockies.

Days Out Ltd
Tel: 0115 941 9330/0115 948 4525
UK tours from this company include such treats as the 'Lincolnshire Poacher', the Blackpool Tower express and Shap Time Trials.

Fantastic Aussie Tours
Tel: (Australia code) 047 82 1866
Operates return steam trips into the Blue Mountains, inland from Sydney, using gorgeous streamlined steam locomotives.

GW Travel Ltd
Tel: 0161 928 9410
Splendid steam tours from this company, including the 'Trans-Siberian', hauled by various exotic locos including the P36 shown on page 12. The trip runs from the Atlantic to the Pacific, across Europe and Asia – all steam-hauled!

Leisurail
Tel: 01733 335599
The UK agent for Australian rail travel that includes such journeys as the six-day 'Sunshine Rail Tour' through Queensland, including the Great Barrier Reef. Also available are useful Austrailpass tickets for individual travellers.

LSW Railtours
Tel: 01543 254076
Based in Hampshire, LSW offers steam excursions with a 'Southern' flavour.

Northumbria Travel
Tel: 01670 829922
The UK agent for Union Limited Steam Safaris in South Africa – vintage locos and unforgettable scenery.

Pathfinder Tours
Tel: 01453 835414
Various UK specials, mostly hauled by steam locos – try the 'Cumbrian Mountain Express', hauled by *Princess Margaret Rose* over the Carlisle & Settle line!

Railway Preservation Society of Ireland
Tel: 01960 353567
Northern Ireland is the stamping ground of the RPSI. Recent trips have included the first special into the new station at Great Victoria Street, Belfast.

Scantours Ltd
Tel: 0171 839 2927
Operates in Scandinavia, with trains that run under such titles as 'The Wilderness Express'. Apart from the rail interest, you can try exotic Scandinavian foods like reindeer, elk, cloudberries and cream!

SNCF Rail Shop
Tel: Bookings 0345 300 003
Information 0891 515 477
French Railways has various offers and packages for the continental rail traveller.

South African Airways Holidays
Tel: 01342 322525
Offers luxury packages that include the 'Blue Train' and the 'Pride of Africa'.

Southern Africa Travel
Tel: 01904 692469
More African rail travel that includes such delights as the Edwardian Safari and Zambezi Special – lots of steam haulage!

Steam & Safaris Ltd
Tel: 01433 620805
Operates a wide range of rail holidays, including China, India, Pakistan, Cuba, USA, South Africa – even Sardinia.

TEFS Ltd
Tel: 01509 262745
China, Ukraine, Vietnam and Turkey are just some of the destinations offered by this Loughborough-based firm.

Venice Simplon-Orient-Express Ltd
Tel: 0171 928 6000
Operates an updated version of the famed journey to Venice by luxury train. Also provides various Pullman trips within the UK and now offers you Far East travel too. The two year old Eastern & Oriental Express service was the first train ever to transport passengers direct from Singapore and Kuala Lumpur to Bangkok, a distance of 1,943 km (1,207 miles).

Waterman Railways
Tel: 01543 419472/254076
'Heritage Days Out' with Waterman include such goodies as a double-header excursion to Penzance.

ABOUT THE AUTHOR

Dave Roberts is a graduate of the University of Birmingham and worked as a curator at the RAF Museum, London, for twelve years. He has translated books and articles from French and German, and has written about vintage aircraft for the *Air Show Guide* from Delta Publishing. His fascination with railways, particularly steam, has been reinforced by the rise of the preservation movement; the new generation of high-speed trains has added an extra dimension to his interest. This is his first major railway reference work.

We welcome ideas and suggestions for inclusion in future editions of this annual. Enquiries to:
Railway Annual
Annuals Publishing Ltd
One High Street
Princes Risborough
Bucks HP27 0AG

Picture right: Class 19D 4-8-2 built by the North British Loco Works in 1948. It is seen here thundering through the Tourwaterspoort Gorge, South Africa, May 1995.